DON'T BELIEVE
YOUR EYES

Published by Lifeway Press ® • © 2021 Brock Gill

ISBN: 978-1-0877-3410-1
Item Number: 005829958

Dewey Decimal Classification Number: 248.83
Subject Heading: RELIGION/Christian Ministry/Youth

Printed in the United States of America.

Student Ministry Publishing
Lifeway Resources
One Lifeway Plaza
Nashville, TN 37234-0144

We believe that the Bible has God for its author; salvation for its end; and truth, without any mixture of error, for its matter and that all Scripture is totally true and trustworthy. To review Lifeway's doctrinal guideline, please visit www.lifeway.com/doctrinalguideline.

Author images courtesy of Elaine Photography

EDITORIAL TEAM

BEN TRUEBLOOD
Director, Student Ministry

JOHN PAUL BASHAM
Manager, Student Ministry Publishing

KAREN DANIEL
Team Leader, Short Term Resources

SCOTT LATTA
Content Editor

MORGAN HAWK
Production Editor

AMY LYON
Graphic Designer

CONTENTS

INTRODUCTION

You have been lied to. It may be hard to believe, but you may have actually been tricked just moments ago. Look back at the cover of this book. Did you catch it?

Your eyes lied to you. Your eyes, in partnership with your brain, read, "Don't Believe Your Eyes." But it doesn't actually say that. Take a third look if you need. Once you see the truth, you're never able to see it wrong again. It's so obvious now. You think, "How could I possibly fall for that?"

I have spent much of my life studying the art of illusion. As a sleight-of-hand artist, I love finding ways to mix psychology and dexterity to trick the eye. The eyes are easily deceived. Through methods of misdirection and the principles of illusion, I have found that it's simple to fool the eye. But what I find most interesting is that it's actually more than the eye itself that is being fooled—it's the brain. The art of perception has become my favorite subject to explore.

Our eyes play tricks on us all the time. But the truth, once you know it, sticks with you. That's the goal of this book. We want you to have an "aha!" moment each week—to see the truth and not be tricked by deception. Our eyes are easily deceived. Our hearts are easily deceived. But the truth of God shines light on our hearts and illuminates the path.

ABOUT THE AUTHOR

Whether riding a motorcycle blindfolded or escaping underwater from a labyrinth of chains, Brock Gill is always living on the edge. Having toured in over 20 countries since 1997, Brock has one clear and evident purpose: sharing the love of Jesus with the forgotten, the broken, and the hopeless.

Brock is the founder of Brock Gill Creative, a nonprofit organization that trains and sends creative evangelists into developing countries to share the gospel. He is the host of the 2006 BBC documentary, *The Miracles of Jesus*, and the author of *Feed the Dog*, released in 2017. His passion is to make sure every person on earth hears this message: "You are loved."

HOW TO USE

In this book, you will find seven weeks of group sessions and personal study. Each session consists of a group guide followed by three days of personal study. As you begin your group time, watch the video for an introduction and illusion performed by author, Brock Gill. There is also a leader guide included in the back of this study with some helpful tips to use during group time. As you close group time, encourage students to complete the personal days that follow the group sessions. Once students have completed this study, they will be able to recognize the lies our culture tells us and replace them with the truth of God's love.

BIBLE STUDY BOOK

Listed below are the different elements in the Bible study book.

Group Discussion

Questions and personal connections are provided to help guide the conversation.

Personal Study

Three days of personal Bible study will help reinforce the theme and provide an opportunity to study passages not covered in the group discussion.

Leader Guide

The leader guide at the back of the study provides ideas for activities and deeper group discussions.

SESSION OUTLINE

Design your group sessions to fit the space, time, and needs of your group. The following is a sample group session outline that you can adapt.

1. Press Play

Review the material in the previous week's personal Bible study and watch the video.

2. Start

Begin the discussion by answering any questions students may have about what Brock shared in the video.

3. Encounter

Foster conversation among the group using the Scripture and discussion questions provided.

4. Connect

Answer some final questions together and spend some time looking at the upcoming personal study days. Close the session with prayer.

Session 1

BROKEN

PRESS PLAY

Watch the Session 1 video. Take notes and list any questions in the space below to discuss after with your group.

START

I was ten years old when I got the news. My parents sat me down and told me we were moving to a new city in a different state. At the time it didn't seem like that big of a deal. I would soon realize I was wrong.

When we moved from our home in Louisiana to a new city, I quickly realized that making friends was difficult. I began to experience loneliness and sadness like I had never experienced before. The next few years were filled with difficult times: I was bullied, made fun of, teased, tricked, and beat up by bigger, more popular kids. I felt the pain of not fitting in.

I tried to hide that I was the new kid who didn't dress or talk the same. But no matter how hard I tried, I still felt like no one loved me and I was broken. I remember many times as a teen having thoughts of suicide and even went as far as making plans to end my own life. I was so broken and felt no hope. I began to believe the lies inside my head that I was worthless, would never amount to anything, that no one cared for me, and that I had no hope of a happy future. I found myself asking the question, "Am I loved?"

> **Have you ever experienced a time in your life where everything was broken?**

> **You don't have to raise your hand—just think about it for a moment. Have you ever felt broken—not good enough, in need of repair, beyond hope?**

We all experience it on some level. A quick glance around the room—maybe even the room you're sitting in right now—will get in your head pretty quickly.

I'm not as pretty as she is.
I'm not as talented as they are.
I'm a mess compared to him.

Turn on the TV—or just wait for an ad to roll—and you'll hear something similar.

Vote for me; I'll fix this.
Buy this product; it'll restore your confidence.
Take this quiz; it will show you where you belong.

In no time flat, you internalize the message: *I am broken.* You might not even notice it always in the background of your mind, coloring your interactions, changing the way you think about yourself. I am broken.

> **What are some ways the world tells us we are broken? What are some ways it promises to fix us?**

For some people, probably even people sitting in this room, you don't have to be told anything to believe that you're broken. You can point to the exact moment in time that you broke. It was something you did. Something someone else did to you. From that point on, you became "that person who _____." That person who is broken.

We're going to look at a woman today who fully believed that she was broken and that she'd live the rest of her life broken. Repair was completely out of the question; she just wanted to survive.

And we're going to see why nothing could have been further from the truth.

ENCOUNTER

>> **Turn to John 4. Have a volunteer read the first six verses out loud.**

To anybody living in Israel at this time, there were two kinds of people: Jews and Gentiles. Jews were people "like them." They had the same stories, the same beliefs, the same things they thought were important. The Gentiles were a little different. Jews avoided Gentiles at all costs. They called them dogs. Unclean.

> **What divisions exist in our world today? In general, how do we see people today treat those who aren't like them?**

John 4:1-6 tells us that in order to get to Galilee, Jesus had to go through Samaria. Israelites were not particularly fond of Samaritans. Samaria had a lot of people who were both Gentile and Jew. To the Jews, Gentiles were dirty—they had Gentile blood. To the Gentiles, Jews were outcasts—they had Jewish blood. They each had their own religion, their own rules, their own temple.

We have a word for the attitude the Jews had for the Samaritans: prejudice. They believed certain things about them regardless of whether or not it was true.

> **Where do we still see prejudice today?**

Keep those people in mind, because Jesus is about to meet someone like that.

>> *Read verses 7-15 aloud.*

Remember what verse 6 told us? It's about noon when this encounter happens. The heat of the day. In Israel.

Every day, in the cool of the morning (usually before the sun came up), women carried big jars to the well in the middle of town to get enough water for the entire day. But not this woman. She waited until the sun was high in the sky, when there would be the fewest number of people around. And she saw a man there. A Jewish man. And he asked her for water.

Already, she was probably internalizing everything she'd come to believe about herself. She was a Samaritan—this Jewish man was probably already looking down on her for that. She was a woman—this Jewish man was definitely looking down on her for that. She had wanted a conflict-free trip to the well, but it was now too late for that. And on top of everything else, he was saying some confusing things.

> **Have one person read the woman's questions and another person read Jesus' responses. What are your reactions to the way He is answering them?**

It had been pleasant up to now. But then things took a turn for the worse. Jesus steered them into the territory that she was desperately hoping to avoid. He reached out and touched the open wound she'd been hiding.

>> *Out loud, continue their conversation by reading verses 16-18.*

> **How does Jesus' statement in verse 16 change the tone of the conversation? How do you think the woman felt talking about this?**

We now see the full picture of what this woman was feeling when she hoped for a hassle-free day of chores. All of her dirty laundry was out in the open. Her brokenness on full display. She was isolated, alone, nursing the hurt of failed relationships.

> **Knowing what you know about this woman, what do you think Jesus' statement in verses 13 and 14 means?**

The woman at the well probably felt her whole life was like a jar with cracks in the sides. She'd keep trying new things to fill herself up, to feel whole, but the water would always spill out. Nothing ever seemed to stick. No number of relationships could fill that void. No number of trips to the well could keep her topped off.

How do you think this woman was trying to fill these "cracks"?

How have you seen people around you trying to fill theirs?

When have you tried to fill yours with something that didn't hold up?

Jesus' answers to the woman's questions might have seemed strange at first. She heard about water that will make you never be thirsty again and she immediately thought of the jar she was holding in her hand. But Jesus was directing her to something bigger than that. He used her physical need for water as an illustration for a bigger need. A spiritual one. She was trying to quench her spiritual thirst with liquid water.

How does Jesus' "Living Water" satisfy us in ways that physical things can't?

What I find beautiful about this story is what happens after the woman encounters Jesus. In verse 28, she leaves her water jar behind, goes back to the city, and tells everyone about the man she just met. They all come to see Jesus and many become followers of the Savior of the world.

He offers the same thing to us that He offered to her: living water, more powerful than the brokenness we feel, more potent than the empty things we try to fill ourselves up with. There is no brokenness that Jesus is not equipped to handle.

CONNECT

There are two different people sitting in this room: those who haven't received the water Jesus gives and those who have.

For those in the first group, you are going to get to see Jesus first-hand over the next seven weeks. You will get to walk alongside Him and see how He interacts with people who aren't all that different from us. You will get to see how He mends broken people. You will get to taste the kind of water He provides.

For those in the second group, you have an opportunity. You are part of a mended generation made whole by Christ. But that carries some responsibility. It means that you interact with the world around you not as someone broken and in need of repair, but like the person who has found the repair. It changes how you treat the people who are different than you are. It changes the way you view the disadvantaged and downtrodden. It changes the way you see yourself—not as someone broken, but as someone who has been made whole.

> **How does Jesus' encounter with the woman at the well relate to us today?**

> **What do you think a plausible next step for yourself might be, no matter where you are right now?**

In Jeremiah 2:13, Jeremiah says that the people of Israel had committed two evils:

1. *They have forsaken God, the fountain of living waters.*
2. *They have made cisterns for themselves that are broken and can't hold any water.*

When Jesus showed up at the well and met the woman drawing water there in the middle of the day, He found someone who had also done exactly that. She did not know God. Her own personal well was cracked and split and no matter what she did to try to fill it, she was always running on empty.

She is no different than any of us. If there's one thing we're good at, it's trying to fill ourselves up with things that won't satisfy us.

Blaise Pascal was a philosopher who once wrote, in not quite these words:

There is a God-shaped vacuum in the heart of each person which cannot be satisfied by any created thing but only by God the Creator.[1]

> **Does this quote ring true to you? Why or why not?**

> **What are things that you use to try to fill this vacuum?**

God created us to have community with Him. He wants us to know Him, to walk with Him, to love Him. He gave us that "vacuum" because it reminds us that we need Him constantly. He's the only one who fits there. But when we start trying to put other things in the place He should be, it is easy for us to give in to the overwhelming thought: I am broken.

> **On a scale from 1-10, with 1 being "not at all" and 10 being "completely," how broken do you feel you are?**
>
>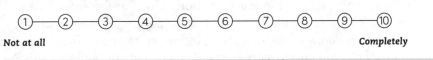
>
> **Not at all**   **Completely**

> **Why do you feel that way?**

Different people will answer this question differently for a billion different reasons. For some, it's because of something that happened to you, or it's because of something you've done. For others, it's that you always feel as though you have an itch in the back of your soul that you can't scratch. Drugs don't scratch it. Relationships don't scratch it. Popularity and a following don't scratch it. You get everything you want and none of it ever seems to complete you.

Jesus knows this about us. He knows how we're wired. He understands that we're going to try to throw anything we can at that hole to putty it over when all we need to do is let Him take it over. Let Him be what He said He was: a fountain of living water that will make you never thirst again.

> **Search your own heart. How can you pray today that Jesus would fill the hole that tells you you're broken?**

1. Blaise Pascal, *Pensées* (New York; Penguin Books, 1966), p. 75.

Have you ever been downtown in the busiest part of your city and watched the way people move on the sidewalks? It is fascinating to watch because just about everywhere, the same things happen: people gather and wait at crosswalks. They walk faster when the crossing hand starts blinking. And they tend to swerve out of the way when they see someone sitting on a stoop, cup on the ground, asking for money.

If you had been around 2,000 years ago, you would have noticed something similar with a specific group of people. The lepers. Lepers were people who had contagious skin diseases and, to put it frankly, their lives were terrible.

First of all, they weren't allowed to touch anybody else. For the entire time they were sick, they couldn't experience the touch of another person. Second of all, they weren't allowed to take part in any of the activities everyone else could. They were social outcasts. Third of all, whenever people looked at them, it was with disgust. People crossed over to the other side of the street to avoid them.

They were, for all practical purposes, broken.

> *Have you ever felt like a social outcast? What made you feel that way? How did it affect you?*

>> *Open your Bible and read Matthew 8:1-4.*

Notice that there are some very interesting things that happen here. First, a leper walks up to Jesus. Remember what we said above about lepers? They weren't allowed to be anywhere near other people. But this leper walked straight up to Jesus and something important happened: Jesus didn't back away. This leper's brokenness didn't scare Jesus.

Notice the second thing that happened: Jesus reached out and touched him. According to the laws of the day, it was illegal to touch a leper. But the leper's brokenness didn't scare Jesus.

Look at the final thing that happened: the leper was healed. Cured. Whole. He was once again able to visit the temple. He was once again able to rejoin society. He could be around people without them dodging him and looking down on him with scorn. No amount of medical treatments, wishful thinking, or desperation could fill the void in this man's life ... until Jesus came around and made him whole.

This same Jesus is available to you today, waiting for you to do the same thing this leper did.

In the verse below, I want you to put your name in the first blank and then fill in the blank at the end with whatever you feel needs to go there.

> And behold, _____ came to Jesus and knelt before him, saying,
>
> "Lord, if you will, you can make me clean from my _____."

» *Spend a few minutes in prayer asking Jesus to make you clean.*

As part of a mended generation, we have a pretty cool opportunity: we get to demonstrate to a broken world what it looks like when a broken person meets Jesus.

Think back to the woman at the well. She had nothing working in her favor. All of her relationships had failed. Her reputation was in the trash. She wasn't living, she was just *surviving*.

And then she met Jesus. And that's when everything changed.

> **This is just speculation. But what do you think her life was like after she met Jesus? How do you think her opinion of herself changed?**

It's not a stretch to say that brokenness is rampant in the world around us. But we don't have to be part of the brokenness, part of the darkness. Instead, we can stand with flashlights in our hands to point people toward the only one who can make us whole. The only one who can satisfy.

Take a look at some of the ways the world around us is broken. How have you seen each of these in your own life? What do you think that we, as believers, can do to address it?

>> **Racism**

>> **Addiction**

>> **Depression**

>> **Violence**

>> **Tragedy**

The first step, before we can do any of this, is to address the central lie at the heart of this issue: *I am broken.*

Jesus came to make sure that you know the opposite is true. You are not broken. You are so much more than that: you are loved. And the one who loves you most is already here, already capable, already standing and waiting for you to ask, as the leper did in yesterday's study, for Him to make you whole.

Session 2

BRAND

PRESS PLAY

Watch the Session 2 video. Take notes and list any questions in the space below to discuss after with your group.

START

What are some of your favorite brands? What feelings do you associate with them?

Think about the word *Nike* for a second. What comes to mind?

Some immediately see shoes: high top Jordans or sleek cross trainers. Some think of the iconic swoosh. For others, it's not so much one image, but a host of them: practice fields and tennis courts, tournaments and sports drinks.

Nike has spent billions of dollars crafting a brand: the associations that come to mind when you hear their name or see their product on a shelf. They want to control the kinds of things you think about when you see their logo or name.

Of course, products you see in a store aren't the only things that get branded. Anything that comes to you from someone else—whether it's a source of information, a musical artist, a production studio, or an organization—has probably been branded. A brand is a reputation.

In fact, the thing that tends to get branded more than anything else is us. We want to control what people think of us when we're not in the room. We want to become associated with only certain types of words. Certain kinds of posts. Certain positive emotions.

In what ways do you see people trying to "brand" themselves?

What tools do people use to craft their own brand?

I've interviewed and worked with many famous people. I often notice the people who have a brand strategy: They spend a lot of time and energy developing and strengthening their brand. And I also notice that they have become a brand that is sometimes very different than the true person they are.

Brand coaches promise to help you "strengthen" your brand. Sometimes this is a good business move. But sometimes it is detrimental to us as people. As someone who is in the public eye and works on stage, I have had to face the reality of this tension. The key for me has been to remain pure, not a manufactured brand that is something I am not. I am just me. I have to separate the business side of Brock Gill from the person Brock Gill. I have to ignore the praise or criticism I get on social media and see things through the eyes of my creator and savior. I have to remember not to believe my own eyes but know that I am a husband, a friend, a son, and a child of God. That's what truly matters.

Here's the thing: our brand, our reputation, is important to us. But sometimes, that can get in the way of us finding what is truly important. And that struggle is nothing new. In fact, Jesus had an encounter with someone struggling with that exact thing—and the way He handled it will show us a lot about how we should think of ourselves.

ENCOUNTER

>> *Turn to John 3 and have someone read the first three verses out loud.*

If there's something that biblical writers were good at, it's packing a lot of information into just a couple of words. These three verses give us a whole lot of information.

1. **We know that Nicodemus was a Pharisee.** Pharisees were the classic know-it-alls. You have a question? Pharisees have an answer. You have a problem? Pharisees have a solution. They were super educated, super opinionated, and super set in their ways.

2. **We know that Nicodemus was a ruler.** He wasn't just an ordinary guy. He had a reputation, and he had power. He was rich with money and with influence.

3. **He was curious, and he was nervous to approach Jesus.** Verse 2 shows us that Nicodemus came to Jesus at night. This is huge. He didn't approach Him with a question during the day, when everyone could see Him; he waited until nighttime when Jesus was probably alone. He didn't just ignore Jesus and avoid Him altogether; he couldn't help but approach Jesus with questions.

> Why do you think this Pharisee waited until nighttime to seek Jesus out?

> What do you think Nicodemus had to lose by being associated with Jesus?

> What do you think you—or someone like you—have to lose by being associated with Jesus?

For Nicodemus, his entire reputation—his entire brand—was at stake. Everything he had worked for, everything he had studied for, everything he had spent years building. All of it. But he still had some nagging questions about what Jesus had been talking about, and it bothered him so much that he just had to do something about it. There was something about Jesus that drew him in.

>> *Have someone read John 3:4-9 out loud.*

> If you could pick anything, what would you want to be known for? What do you think it would take to get that kind of reputation?

Nicodemus's whole reputation centered around how smart he was. He was a teacher. A ruler. He was the one people went to when they had questions, because they knew that he had the answers.

But now he was coming to find Jesus in the dead of night because he couldn't help but feel like there was something he was missing. He controlled everything about the way that people saw him, but it still left him feeling unsatisfied.

What picture can you remember "liking" yesterday on Instagram. None? Must not have been very impactful. You didn't really "like" it, as much as you were sending a message to the person saying, "Hey, I 'liked' it. I came to your space and saw something. Notice that I did that." An Instagram expert probably told you to "like" everything as a way to be seen and noticed when you were just beginning to use the app. Maybe they should rename the button "notice me," because we are really just wanting to be seen and acknowledged. And again we are asking, "Am I loved?"

Since so much of our lives has moved online, it has never been easier to try to shape what people think of us. To curate our image. To untag ourselves from photos we don't think are flattering and only post the highlights.

A few years ago, one Instagram influencer was sick of this, so she changed her account's name to "Social Media Is Not Real Life." She edited the captions of her photos to say things like, "NOT REAL LIFE - took over 100 in similar poses trying to make my stomach look good. Would have hardly eaten that day. Would have yelled at my little sister to keep taking them until I was somewhat proud of this. Yep so totally #goals."[1]

> How is it easy to use social media to control the way people see us?

All of Nicodemus's image-control did nothing to fill the hole inside of him. Even though he knew to seek out Jesus, these verses showed us that, even after Jesus started talking, Nicodemus still didn't understand. He was stuck in his old way of thinking. He was still Nicodemus the teacher. Nicodemus the ruler. Nicodemus the answer-haver.

So look at how Jesus brought him close.

>> *Have someone read John 3:14-18 out loud.*

> **Have you heard any of these verses before? What do they mean to you?**

Wrapped up in this section is probably the most famous Bible verse in the entire world—but it is even cooler than you think it is. Think about this for a second.

Nicodemus was a teacher of the Law. That meant that he was an expert in the books we call the Old Testament. But this time, he wasn't teaching a lesson from the Old Testament, Jesus was.

In Numbers 21, God sent poisonous snakes into the Israelite camp to punish them for their constant complaining against Him. But then He did something pretty cool. He gave them a way out. Numbers 21:8 says, "Then the Lord said to Moses, 'Make a snake image and mount it on a pole. When anyone who is bitten looks at it, he will recover.'"

>> *Have someone read Numbers 21:4-9 out loud to get the bigger context.*

> **How do you see this story connect with what Jesus told Nicodemus?**

Do you see what Jesus did? He used something that Nicodemus knew, something from his world, and showed him where He fit inside of it. Even though Nicodemus had built what he might have thought was the perfect life, he had missed something important: Jesus.

Jesus also showed him that everything he had done was not quite enough. He had to be born again. He had to start over, and this time, build his life right: not with the best image he could make of himself, but one that looked more and more like Christ every day.

CONNECT

We are professionals at making our lives look as good as we can possibly make them look. But if we were actually doing a good job, we wouldn't look all around us and see so many people hurting. Insecure. Ashamed. Faking it.

But Jesus gave us an opportunity to change everything. To be born again, a new person under His brand. Five times in three verses, he told Nicodemus that it all hinges on one thing: believing in Him. You are not a brand. But you are loved so much that someone else died so that you could join His. All He asks from you is that you believe in Him.

> **Do you see yourself in Nicodemus's story?**

> **What is one thing you feel like you could change in your life today?**

1. Adrienne Cutway, "Teen Instagram Star Quits Social Media Claiming 'It's Not Real Life,'" *The Morning Call*, November 3, 2015, https://www.mcall.com/os-teen-instagram-star-quits-social-media-20151103-post.html.

Every now and again, companies do what is called a "brand analysis."

A brand analysis tries to answer one question: "How do your customers feel about you?" They do this by asking a few questions like these:

What are we producing?
What kind of customers are we trying to reach?
How are we, as a brand, coming across to those customers?

It isn't just companies that do this, though. We tend to do the same things. We want to know what it is that we're known for. How we're coming across to the people around us. What kinds of people we're trying to impress.

We learned about Nicodemus this week, and how he was so busy defining himself that he didn't stop to consider what Jesus had to say about him.

On your own, do a little bit of a "personal brand analysis."

What would you say your "brand" is? What do you think you're known for?

What would you say your reputation is? How do you think people perceive you?

What are things that you do to "keep up" your brand?

In 2017, the most popular paid app in the App Store was one called Facetune: an app that lets users edit their photos easily and quickly.[1] It removes blemishes. Fixes jaw lines. Improves complexions. The app quickly became worth over $1 billion.[2]

It's safe to say that we, as a society, are very good at going to great lengths to adjust the way we come across to other people. We want to look our best. Say our best. Feel our best. And, for a lot of us, we put in serious work to make that happen.

But it's easy for "putting on our best face" to become an obsession. Soon, it starts to affect the way we feel about ourselves—like we're somehow less if we don't reach some standard that we've set for ourselves.

> *How important is it to you that people see only your good side?*

> *What lengths do you go to in order to make sure that is the only side of you people see?*

We already looked at Nicodemus, but this week we're going to see someone else who built a brand out of himself. Unlike Nicodemus, though, he didn't exactly handle it the same way. What we need to understand is how important our own image, whether it is how successful we are or how beautiful we look or how put-together we appear, is to us.

Then, once we figure out how much that influences the way we see ourselves, we can see how there's something even better for us than we could dream up on our own.

1. Karissa Bell, "Apple's Most Downloaded Apps of 2017," *Mashable*, December 7, 2017, https://mashable.com/2017/12/07/apple-most-popular-iphone-apps-2017/.

2. Connie Loizos, "The Maker of Popular Selfie App Facetune Just Landed $135 Million at a Unicorn Valuation," *Tech Crunch*, July 31, 2019, https://tcrn.ch/319SSF5.

You've probably heard someone ask at some point, "If you had to leave your house right this second and could only take one thing, what would it be?"

People have all sorts of answers. A laptop. An expensive watch. I know someone whose father has a box labeled "grab in case of fire" in the garage. It is filled with Christmas ornaments.

> *What would be the one thing you would grab if you had to leave in a hurry? Why is it so important to you?*

We all have things that are important to us, that we wouldn't want to live without. But I want to ask a little bit of a different question:

> *What would you be willing to give up if Jesus asked you to?*

It hits a little bit harder, doesn't it?

Instead of answering right away, let's look at someone else who was asked this question, see what his response was, and figure out if it still applies to us.

>> *Open up your Bible and read Mark 10:17-22.*

Let's be real: sometimes it is difficult to read something that was written a long time ago and relate to it. It was a different time, they were different people, and they had different struggles and problems than we do today.

Then there are encounters like this that feel ... almost modern. You could imagine it happening on the street right in front of you. A man comes up to Jesus and asks what seems to be a simple question.

But we all know what kind of question this was. It wasn't an honest one. This man

wasn't looking for an answer, he was looking for affirmation. He wanted Jesus to look at him and say, "Whoa. You're awesome. You have kept the law! You have gotten wealthy! You're good to go, man."

That's why Jesus poked him in a sore spot. In his wallet. In his reputation.

In his brand.

Jesus wasn't telling him that it's bad to be rich or popular or put-together. That wasn't the point at all. What He did was expose the man's heart. He made the man prove what was most important to him. It wasn't heaven, it wasn't God's kingdom, it wasn't following Jesus. It was what he had made for himself.

I think it's interesting that Jesus' pitch was always the same: "Come follow me." Simple. Straight to the point. Perfectly clear.

But it can be so, so difficult. Following Jesus means that He is on the throne of your heart. He's the one leading the way, and you're the one following.

> **How did the man in the story demonstrate what the most important thing in his life was?**

> **What is the most important thing in your life?**

> **Think about the question at the beginning of this study: What would you be willing to give up to follow Jesus?**

When a king would send a letter a long time ago, he would seal it with wax and stamp it with his ring. That ring was one of a kind, and when it pressed into the wax, it would prove a couple of things.

>> First, it would prove that it was the king who sent it.

>> Second, it would prove that the king approved of what was inside.

>> Third, it made whatever the letter contained official. You knew exactly who it belonged to.

Genesis 1:26 tells us that God made us in His image. That means that from the moment we're born, we look like God does. We have all of the stuff that points people back to Him. We are stamped with His approval. Signed with His seal.

But the more we try to make an image of ourselves—the more we try to brand ourselves in a way that makes us look the best—the less we look like the one who made us.

You know the little icons on your phone that open up different apps? That's sort of what people are. We're shortcuts to something else. What we have to decide is what we want people to see when they look at us.

Do we want them to see a super put-together person with great fashion sense? Someone who everyone wants to be like? Those aren't bad things by themselves, but if that's all we are, we're missing what God made us to be.

He made us to be lighthouses that point other people back to Him. To be seals on a letter He sent the world. To be adventurers sent out to tell everyone else about a kingdom so much bigger than any kingdom the world has ever known.

How do you think someone pointing back to God would interact with people they don't agree with?

How do you think someone pointing back to God would interact with their friends? Their family?

How well do you think you match that description?

What is one thing you need to work on changing this week?

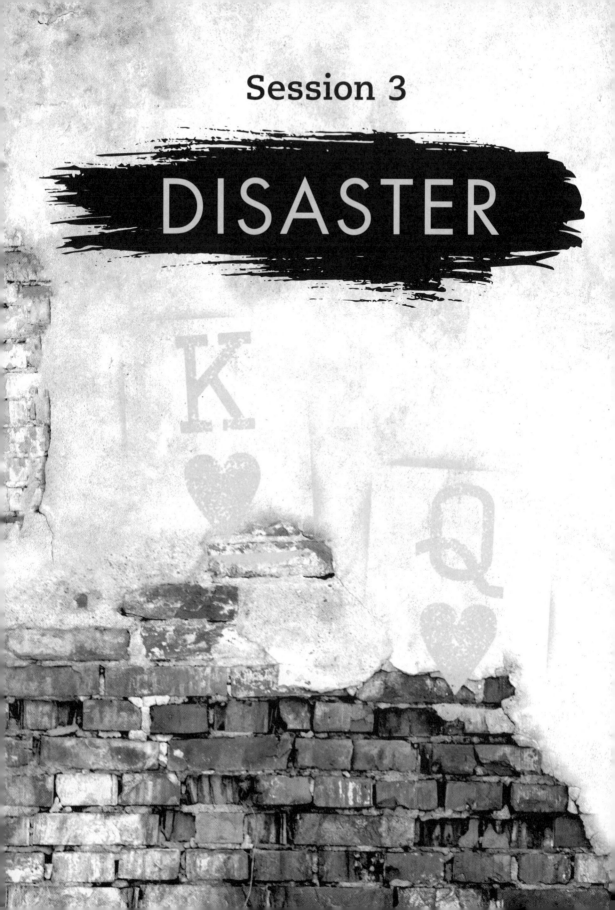

Session 3

DISASTER

PRESS PLAY

Watch the Session 3 video. Take notes and list any questions in the space below to discuss after with your group.

START

Every year, I spend time in Greece doing shows and sharing the love of Jesus with refugees. On my most recent visit, I met a man who will forever be in my memory. He approached me on the street near a refugee community and humbly asked me for money. At first I hesitated, but in my hesitation, I had a chance to look into his eyes. What I saw was true desperation.

Just a few weeks before, this man was in his home country of Syria living in a nice neighborhood, driving a nice car, and working a great job as a pharmacist. He had a master's degree and was from a successful family. One day, while he was at home with his wife and two children, a rocket hit his house. He and his family fled with nothing but the clothes on their backs. After paying a smuggler his last dime, he found his way into Greece. Now he was homeless and sleeping on a park bench with his wife and kids.

Sometimes, it's our choices that lead to consequences in our lives. And sometimes, it's the things we can't control that leave our lives in shambles.

> **Has there ever been a time when uncontrollable circumstances set your life on a course you couldn't control?**

> **Have you ever felt like life wasn't going how it was supposed to be?**

My life is nothing like it was supposed to be.

Is this you? You feel like you had dreams and a plan that just didn't pan out. You were on the right track, but at some point things just changed. What's worse is that you don't even know how.

I started with so much potential, but look at how I've wasted it.

Maybe this is you: you can identify the exact moment when things went wrong. And you feel like you know exactly who is at fault. It's you. You made the decision. You said the words. You ignored the warning signs.

It leads you like a spider down the drain to the conclusion:

I am a full-on disaster.

> **Have you ever known someone with this mentality? Have you ever felt it?**

If you have ever felt like this, you're far from alone. Let's look at a time when Jesus talked with someone who probably felt the same way.

ENCOUNTER

>> *Have a volunteer read Luke 19:1-5 out loud.*

Let's talk about traitors. Let's say you have a friend that you tell a secret to. You're hurting, you're sad, you're desperate for someone to listen to you. You're getting something off your chest, knowing that your friend is going to keep your secret, console you, and tell you they have your back.

They do all of that. They tell you that you're safe with them. That you can trust them.

If you showed up the next day and that person had told everyone your secret, you'd be angry. Hurt. Betrayed. The trust you put in that friend was turned against you.

> **Have you ever felt like someone betrayed your trust? How did it make you feel about that person?**

> **How do you think they feel about what they did?**

That person is Zacchaeus. Zacchaeus was a Jewish man. He was supposed to look out for his fellow Jews. What he did was the exact opposite.

Zacchaeus was a tax collector. Tax collectors were usually Jewish citizens who went to work for the Roman government, who promised them that they would get rich. They had a certain amount of money that they had to take in the form of taxes, but there wasn't any law that said they could only take that amount. The law only said that Rome had to get its fair share of money from the Jewish citizens; anything above that, the tax collector could put straight in his own pocket.

And that is what a lot of tax collectors did. They'd grab as much money as they could from as many people as they could get it from, so the Jewish people hated them. When we see that Zacchaeus was a chief tax collector and that he was rich, we can know almost exactly how he got there. From selling out his brothers and sisters.

Imagine what it was like for Zacchaeus to walk down the street. The kinds of looks that he got. What people would say behind his back. It's difficult to imagine, but he probably felt lonely, like he didn't matter to anyone except the officials he owed money to.

Yes, as a tax collector, he might have felt like he brought it on himself, but that is the point. Zacchaeus walked around with this flooding his mind:

I have sold out my own people and I can't stop. Everyone hates me, and it is my fault. I am a complete disaster.

> **Imagine you are a Jew in this time. How would you feel if you saw Zacchaeus walking toward you?**

> **Imagine you are Zacchaeus. How do you think you felt about yourself?**

But one day, something changed. He heard whispers about a religious man who didn't hang out with the rest of the religious people. Instead, He hung out with the people nobody wanted to be around. The lepers. The prostitutes. The tax collectors. What's more, Zacchaeus heard about what this person did when He got around them. He healed them. He forgave them. He restored them.

Zacchaeus knew all at once that he had to get close to this person. He had to see what He looked like, what He sounded like. He had to see if He was real.

But Zacchaeus had a problem. Whenever this man would come into town, He had people around Him all the time. And Zacchaeus was short. What's more, the people all around him couldn't stand him. So he did the only thing he could think of: he climbed a tree.

> **Who is someone you would absolutely love to meet? Why?**

Zacchaeus got up in the tree and then the strangest thing happened. The person he climbed up to see knew his name. He called out to him!

Think about that for a second. Zacchaeus didn't have a single friend in this town. It was worse than that: everyone in this town couldn't stand him. They knew he was a disaster—he was too far gone and no one wanted anything to do with him.

And then Jesus called him by name. Looked at him up in the tree and said, "Hi, Zacchaeus. I'd like to come to your house for dinner. Why don't you come down?"

> **How do you think this made Zacchaeus feel? Excited? Nervous? Anxious? Why do you think so?**

>> *Have a volunteer read verses 6-10 out loud.*

We know exactly how he felt. He was joyful. Jesus did something that nobody had done for a long time, not even Zacchaeus himself. Jesus looked at him and said, "You matter. You are not a disaster, and I can't wait to hang out with you."

He actually even went further than that. Verse 9 shows us how Jesus restored Zacchaeus by saying something specific. "He too is a son of Abraham."

Think of how wild that is. In Jesus' eyes, this complete outcast, this traitor, this sellout, still belongs. What's more, he still belongs because of what Jesus says in verse 10: he's the exact kind of person that Jesus was looking for.

> **Have you ever felt ostracized—intentionally ignored or outcast? How did it make you feel?**

> **Have you ever felt included in something? How did that make you feel?**

Zacchaeus's whole life changed in an instant. All it took was for Jesus to look at him, call him by name, and remind him that there's no such thing as a disaster whenever He gets involved. Another person in the Bible has a similar story: Paul was a religious leader who made it his mission to kill Christians—until he met Jesus. From then on, his whole life was different. He wasn't a disaster, either.

There's no such thing as a disaster whenever Jesus gets involved.

CONNECT

Some of you might feel like Zacchaeus. You might feel like you've done enough bad stuff that there is no way you can ever recover from it. Others might feel like the Israelites who got swindled by Zacchaeus: that some people are just too far gone. They're mean and nasty and selfish and cruel.

In this one encounter, Jesus changed multiple people. He changed Zacchaeus, who promised to repay the people he ripped off four times as much as he took. He changed the people looking on, who got to see firsthand that there's no such thing as someone who is too much of a disaster to be shown kindness and love.

And He can change you, too, regardless of which person you are.

> What is something you are feeling the Holy Spirit telling you to do right now?

> How can you put together a plan to make that happen starting right now?

Have you ever looked at someone else and thought, *how in the world do they do it?*

They have it all together. They are talented and smart. Funny and cool. Successful. Popular. Kind. The actual whole package. It's like everything they touch turns to gold.

And then you catch a glimpse of yourself in the mirror. You only see things that you don't like. You keep missing homework assignments and saying the wrong thing. Your brain feels like it's all over the place. Like the hits start and they don't stop, and no matter where you go, a cloud follows you.

You might find yourself asking, "How in the world could this spiral have gotten so out of hand? And what can I do to just make it stop?"

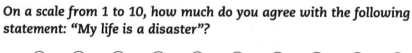

On a scale from 1 to 10, how much do you agree with the following statement: "My life is a disaster"?

①—②—③—④—⑤—⑥—⑦—⑧—⑨—⑩

Is not a disaster   *Is a disaster*

Why did you put that number?

Whenever I think about people whose lives felt out of control, like chaos seemed to follow them and nothing ever went right, I think about a group of people in the Old Testament called the prophets.

A prophet is just someone who takes a message from God to the people who need to hear it. But when Israel was at its peak, God had a lot of things to say to them. And not all of it was positive. For the people He asked to deliver the message, they had it rough.

>> *In your Bible, read 1 Kings 19:1-13.*

Elijah was one of these prophets. Look at where this part of the story starts: he is on the run for his life. Powerful people literally want him dead. He has seen the chaos that followed him, and eventually, he has had enough. Read again what he did in verse 4: He sat down under a tree and asked God to kill him. He wanted it all to be over. He was tired and beaten down and felt stuck in the endless cycle of bad that seemed to follow him everywhere he went.

Elijah was done. He was over it. But look at what God did. He didn't give a lecture, He didn't judge or punish him for those thoughts. He sent an angel to bring him food. That's it. That's all Elijah could even do. Sit and eat.

Eventually, when he had enough strength, Elijah went up on a mountain and asked to see God's presence to get a reminder of why he was doing what he was doing.

» So God sent a tornado. Chaos. Destruction. But that's not where God was.

» Then God sent an earthquake. More chaos. Again, that's not where God was.

» Then God sent a raging fire. But that's not where God was, either.

It wasn't until things calmed down, until Elijah was nursed back to health and safe and secure and quiet that He found out where God was. God was in the soft whisper.

Your life might feel like that raging wind, the earthquake, the fire. You might feel like Elijah did at the beginning, asking God to just come and take you away from it all.

But God has so much more in store for you. Maybe what it will take for you is what it took for Elijah: you have to sit. Be still. Don't do anything; just be. Look at the tornado that your life has become and know that underneath it all, when that tornado goes away, there will be a soft voice whispering to you.

That's where God is. That's where He'll meet you. That's where He'll show you how much He loves you.

> *Take five minutes right where you are and sit quietly. Your head will be filled with thoughts and troubles and worries, and that's OK. Just sit with it. No sound, nothing to read, nothing but you and five minutes of silence. Because in the silence is where you will hear God the loudest.*

Most of us hope that we get remembered for who we were at our best. Sure, we may not change the world and we might not build an empire, but we want those who think back on us to do it with a smile.

> **What do you hope you get remembered for?**

In John 8, we are going to meet someone who was facing what might be some people's worst-case scenario.

>> *In your Bible, read John 8:2-11.*

Imagine being the woman in this encounter. You've been caught red-handed in an act of adultery. You know what is supposed to happen to people caught in adultery because it has been spelled out for you in the law: both of you get stoned to death. You're staring straight at the people who want you to be killed, and you know that when you do, you're going to always be remembered as "that woman who was killed for committing adultery." It will haunt your name forever.

But notice what I said the penalty for adultery was: both of you were to be put to death. Right now, however, you're all alone. That's because this is not about justice; you're just being used as a trap. These religious leaders are using your situation to try to trick Jesus into saying the wrong thing. So now you're feeling responsible for both your own fate and, potentially, His.

Being dragged through the street and having your sin put on display, it's pretty safe to say you're feeling like only one thing: a disaster. Your own life is ruined. Someone else's life might be ruined, too. You are the victim of a political trap. You're being abused by the people who were supposed to protect you.

You look at Jesus with a mix of shame and pleading. You are sorry. You're embarrassed. You're desperate.

>> *Now look at what Jesus did starting in verse 6.*

Nothing. He heard what you did perfectly well, but He just started drawing in the dirt with His finger. And then He looked these religious leaders straight in the eye and said to them that the person without sin—the person who is better than you are—should be the first one to cast the stone.

Imagine the mood of that street that day—the pin-drop silence as the Pharisees dropped their stones and walked away.

Then, after they've left, Jesus—this famous teacher—makes a joke. "Well? Where is everyone? Did nobody condemn you?"

When you say, "I guess not," He says, "Well, I don't either."

Even on her most disastrous day, Jesus looked at this woman with compassion. With forgiveness. With peace. That's what Jesus does. He's a professional at seeing people who are at their worst and treating them like they're at their best. With nothing but some doodles in the dirt and a well-timed sentence, He turned her condemnation into freedom.

And He's more than capable of doing the same for you.

Whatever you're struggling with, no matter what demons from your past you're battling, there is someone bent over in the dirt, on your level, looking at you with compassion. He's holding His hand out to you and saying, "I don't condemn you, either."

> **What is a decision you've made that you feel like you just can't get away from?**

> **What is something that you need to ask Jesus to forgive you of?**

I'm sorry to tell you, but there's never going to come a day when you stop messing up. It's one of the things that we're best at.

I'm also sorry to tell you, but there's not going to be a day when bad stuff stops happening, either. Sometimes, that is just how it goes. Nothing and nobody is perfect.

But none of this defines you. Some of you are going through more difficult things than I can even imagine. You're facing things that I wouldn't wish on anyone. But you are not those things.

When we looked at Elijah and saw that he was on the run for his life, he wasn't running because of something that was his fault. He was just doing what God told him to do. But that didn't stop him from feeling like he was better off dead.

Or maybe you feel like someone else who felt something similar. Read the words that David wrote in Psalm 42:9-11:

> Why must I go about in sorrow because of the enemy's oppression?
> My adversaries taunt me, as if crushing my bones, while all day long they say to me, "Where is your God?"
> Why, my soul, are you so dejected? Why are you in such turmoil?

Have you ever felt like any of the things David said? Oppressed? Taunted? Crushed? Depressed?

What led you to feeling that way?

Even if you haven't felt exactly the thing that David—or Elijah—described, you have probably felt shades of it. Or you will.

And when you do, I have some good news for you: I left off a little bit of that verse. The very end. Because at the end of explaining the way that he felt, David actually showed us his response to it. And it still fits today. Look at the end of verse 11:

Put your hope in God, for I will still praise him, my Savior and my God.

God loves you exactly how you are. He has shown over and over how badly He wants to lift you up, to set you on your feet, to make you feel peace and hope.

He wants you to know beyond a doubt that you are not a disaster.

You are loved.

> **What do you think you would say to someone who feels like they are a disaster?**

> **How can you use some of what you have learned in this session to help someone close to you?**

> **What do you need today in order to do what David said: "Put your hope in God"?**

Session 4

INVISIBLE

PRESS PLAY

Watch the Session 4 video. Take notes and list any questions in the space below to discuss after with your group.

START

When I was a sophomore in college, I accidentally signed up for an upper-level business class. The second I walked in, I noticed all the other students were seniors. I began to get a sick feeling in my stomach and felt very uncomfortable and out of place.

The professor walked to the front of the class and began to lecture. I was lost. Then he divided us into groups of four. Once we were in our groups, he instructed us to create a semester-long project. As my fellow students began to delegate the various responsibilities, I knew I was in way over my head. I had never had any other business course to prepare me for this. My internal voice began to scream, "Run! Just get out!" I wished in that moment that I could be invisible. I was embarrassed and scared. At the end of that class, I ran out and never returned.

Sometimes I wish I could be invisible. (I am an illusionist, after all. I can see some benefits.) But becoming invisible isn't a blessing. It's a curse.

> **Has there ever been a time, even if it's now, when you've felt invisible?**

Tell me if this describes you.

You wake up each morning a little bit disappointed. You have to face the same problems you always do. The same people. The same disrespect.

You have ideas that you feel like nobody wants to hear. Dreams you don't think you'll see play out. Thoughts you'd like to express, goals you'd like to reach, issues you'd like to solve.

But you feel like nobody listens to you. Nobody sees you.

Maybe it's even worse than that. It's that people see you—they know you're there, they interact with you, but it's always negative. You're in the way. You're an obstacle. You're treated like a burden instead of a person.

Maybe you've been rejected or shunned. Or maybe you find yourself in the halls at school or in your own home thinking, *If only someone could see me for what I am.*

You feel invisible.

> **Is there someone in your life who you think might feel this way?**

> **Can you try to put some words to the way it feels?**

If you have ever felt anything like this, you are so far from the only one. In fact, Jesus did something incredible for someone exactly like you.

Today, we're going to see a woman who most definitely felt these things. Maybe you'll be able to relate to the way she felt: discarded, disregarded, alone. Invisible.

And then, maybe you'll see the kind of hope that Jesus offers.

ENCOUNTER

Today's passage starts in the middle of a stressful situation. And the writer, Luke, included some details to help us feel just how stressful it was. Pay attention to the things he includes to show the stress everyone was feeling.

>> *Have a volunteer read Luke 8:40-48 out loud.*

> **Pay attention to verses 42 and 45. What words did Luke include to tell you how chaotic this situation was?**

> **What was going on at the very beginning of this passage? What problem were they dealing with before the sick woman touched Jesus?**

Luke went pretty far out of his way to show the chaos of this scene. There is a desperate man whose daughter is dying. There's a crowd so thick and so close together that they were "nearly crushing" Jesus.

So when this woman reaches out and touches Jesus, no one would have noticed. But Jesus did.

Your Bible probably says that she had "suffered from bleeding for twelve years." When we read that, it doesn't tell us much. But Luke's audience would have understood what he meant. One passage in the Old Testament can help us.

>> **Have a volunteer read Leviticus 15:25-28 out loud. Pay special attention to the things that she touches.**

When Leviticus tells you someone is "unclean," that doesn't mean "sinful." All it means is that they have to go through a process before they can re-enter society. If someone was bleeding or had a skin disease, they would be considered "unclean" and kept away from others because they could spread the disease.

The problem here is that this woman had been bleeding for twelve years. It was a serious problem for her health, but also for her place in society.

> **What do you think this woman's daily life looked like?**

> **How do you think the people around her treated her?**

Try to imagine how frustrating and isolated she had felt for these twelve years. No doctor could help her. No family could touch her. Mark tells us she had spent everything to try to get better, but it was all for nothing. Nothing could fix her.

But then she heard about Jesus. She heard what people were saying about how He could do amazing things like make diseases go away just by touching them.

She also heard that people were calling Him the Son of God. And that probably struck a chord with her, because she heard about what the Son of God would do. She remembered what Malachi said about Him:

> "But for you who fear my name, the sun of righteousness will rise with healing in its wings, and you will go out and playfully jump like calves from the stall" (Mal. 4:2).

Because of this verse and a few others like it, Rabbis would wear long shawls over their bodies with little strings tied to each of the corners. These corners where the strings were tied were literally called the "wings."

With this in mind, reread Luke 8:43-45. What happened after she touched Jesus' robe? How did Jesus react? How did the disciples react? How did the woman react?

Think about how wild this is for a second. An incurably sick woman was at the end of her rope. Neglected, forgotten, invisible.

But she knew that they were calling this man the Son of God. So she did something amazing: She put as much faith as she had in as much of Jesus as she knew. And that was enough. She was cured immediately.

That is amazing. But what is most interesting is what happens next. The woman was so used to being invisible that she immediately shrank back. Even when Jesus asked who it was that touched Him, she didn't speak up. She had gone back to the invisibility she understood, but Jesus wasn't going to keep her there.

Reread verses 46-48. What emotions do you think the woman was feeling when Jesus spoke to her?

What do you think Jesus meant by "your faith has saved you"?

What do you think the people surrounding Jesus thought of this exchange?

Jesus shows us two important things in this encounter. First, He shows us what kind of faith He is looking for. He's not looking for theologians and pastors and people who have it all together—He's looking for people like this woman. Like Zacchaeus. People who are hurting, broken, scared, but who are brave enough to squeeze any amount of faith out of their tired hearts and throw it all to Him.

But the second thing He shows us is that there is no such thing as invisible when it comes to Him. Anyone who seeks Him will find Him. He will see them. Lift them up. Make them whole. And then He will remind them:

You are not a disaster. You are not broken. You are not invisible. You are loved.

CONNECT

This woman didn't do anything to deserve what had happened to her. She was going to all of the right people, seeing all of the best doctors, spending everything she had to try to get better.

That's how it goes sometimes. You're doing everything right. But you still have that little voice creeping up behind you and whispering that you're not enough. You want to be seen, to be heard, but it doesn't matter: you still feel invisible.

For twelve years, nothing the woman tried helped her—until she met Jesus and He healed her. But He did so much more than that. He gave her a way to be seen again. To be held again. To be loved again.

And He did it because He loved her. All because she mustered all the faith she could and threw it at His feet. That's what He does best. He mends the things that are broken. He gives the invisible a voice. And He can do the same for you.

> **What part of the woman's story do you connect with the most?**

> **Is there something that you feel Jesus calling you to do right now?**

"I feel like nothing I do matters."
"I miss when I used to feel alive."
"People look at me, but I don't think anyone actually sees me."

If you're like me, you've thought these things before. You might be thinking them now. There are so many reasons why you might feel things like this. See if any of these ring true:

1. **You feel like a bystander in everyone else's story.** You are overlooked and picked last. It's like you're a ghost roaming the halls with no motivation or drive. That stuff is for other people.

2. **You try your absolute best.** You're even proud of yourself. You think that you are smart and funny, that you work hard and love other people well. But it all goes unnoticed. You feel like you're the only person in the world paying attention to the great stuff you do, and that's a shame—because you think people would like you if they gave you a chance.

3. **You remember a time when you felt like you were on top of the world.** Things worked out for you. People noticed you, thought you were pretty great. You had motivation and purpose, but then something changed. You now feel aimless, a shell of the person you used to be. All of that great stuff seems sort of like a memory.

> *Did any of these resonate with you? Which one? Why?*

> *If none of them did, is there something else that makes you feel invisible? See if you can put it into words below.*

It's funny—each of us is the main character in a story. It's our story. We know it well—the things that got us to where we are. The plans we hope to accomplish. We know where the conflict is, and who the supporting characters are.

But then we fear that nobody cares about the story we're living. That it doesn't matter to anyone but us.

We feel alone. Isolated. Invisible.

Tomorrow we're going to meet someone else who felt this way and see how God approached her. Because the truth is, every single one of the statements at the beginning of today's study is a lie. You do matter. You are important. You are seen.

And most importantly, above everything else in the world, you are deeply, immeasurably loved.

> **Write down some thoughts you have about feeling isolated, alone, or invisible.**

> **When do you feel that way the most?**

> **When do you feel most seen?**

A guy named Robert Putnam wrote a book called *Bowling Alone*, and in that book he said that the most dangerous issue people today face is loneliness.[1] We're not as social as we used to be. COVID-19 amplified this issue, forcing us to spend months in our houses, away from most of the people that we love.

Loneliness is the kind of thing that will eat at you. It'll keep you up at night. It will start telling you things about yourself that aren't true: that you aren't valuable. That you aren't amazing. That you aren't loved.

> *What is the most alone you have ever felt?*

> *Do you feel alone right now? Lonely? Isolated? Write a few sentences about how you feel.*

Before I have you look something up in your Bible, I need to give you some backstory, because it is a little bit complicated.

Hagar was a servant in Abram's house. But Abram had a problem: He and his wife Sarai weren't able to have any children. So Sarai did something that seems a little crazy: she told Abram to have a baby with Hagar, instead.

It turns out that the idea wasn't a great one (for a lot of reasons). One of those reasons is that when Hagar got pregnant with Abram's child, Sarai started to hate her. Sarai was jealous and angry and bitter. Soon, she started mistreating Hagar, so much so that Hagar eventually ran away.

So here Hagar is, on the run from her employer, carrying his child, completely alone. She can't go somewhere new because she doesn't know anybody. She can't go back to where she was because she would just suffer more abuse. She was stuck in a terrible situation, and she couldn't see any way out of it.

>> *So now, open your Bible and read Genesis 16:7-13.*

> **Pay special attention to verse 13. Who is someone who sees you—really sees you? How does it make you feel to be seen and known and accepted just as you are?**

This encounter was so meaningful to Hagar that she came up with her own special name for God. She called Him "El-roi," which means "the God who sees."

Not only did God see her, but God went out looking for her and found her.

And He is the exact same God who is out looking for you right now. He is El-roi: the God who sees. He sees you for who you are. For who you were. For who you will be. And He is still seeking you out.

Jesus said this exact thing in Luke 19:10: *He came to seek and save the lost.*

Maybe this is you. Maybe you feel like who you are isn't enough. That you aren't valuable or worthwhile or deserving of anything but the loneliness and isolation that you feel all around you. But I have such good news for you: Jesus is alive. He's looking for you. The "God who sees" sees you. And He loves you.

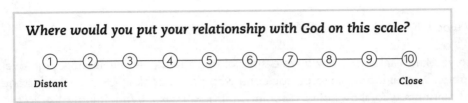

Where would you put your relationship with God on this scale?

①—②—③—④—⑤—⑥—⑦—⑧—⑨—⑩

Distant   **Close**

> **Who is someone you know that might feel invisible? How can you help them know that you see them?**

1. Robert Putnam, *Bowling Alone: The Collapse and Revival of American Community* (New York: Simon & Schuster, 2000).

As we begin, take a few minutes to fill out a short questionnaire:

> **What do you think your best quality is?**

> **When do you feel the most healthy?**

> **When does God feel the most real to you?**

> **What is one thing you hope to accomplish some day?**

> **What is one thing you are most proud of?**

Look back at all the things you wrote down in those spaces.

Each one of them is something that makes you unique. You are a person worth knowing and loving and seeing. They are also things that God sees in you. Do you remember the name that Hagar gave God? El-roi. He is the God who made you. The God who loves you.

The God who sees you.

Because you know this, you now have a special opportunity. A few sessions ago, we talked about what it looks like to be someone who points back to God. An ambassador from His kingdom who shows other people what God is like. What it looks like to be known by Him.

So here's something you can do as someone who knows what it feels like to not be invisible: you can show it to other people. So let's come up with a plan for how you can do that.

> *Who are people you would consider friends? Make a list of the first few who come to mind.*

> *Beside each of their names, write down something you think is special about them and what their best quality is.*

> *For each person on that list, what is something you can do to let them know that they are seen, known, and loved?*

You don't have to come up with an elaborate plan to let someone know that you see them. Sometimes, it's just a random text in the middle of the day that says, "Hey, I just wanted you to know, I think it is so awesome how great you are at _____. It makes me happy to see you happy."

One simple act of making someone feel seen and accepted, even if they already know that you are their friend, can go a long way. And as a representative of El-roi, the God who sees, we have a special opportunity to help other people know that He sees them, too.

PRESS PLAY

Watch the Session 5 video. Take notes and list any questions in the space below to discuss after with your group.

> **Have you ever experienced the feeling of being left behind? What did it feel like?**

If it hasn't happened already, one day you are going to look around at the people you know best and realize that nobody is the same as they used to be. Some of your friends will have new hobbies or interests that don't involve you. They will be taking opportunities that you weren't offered. Going places you weren't invited to.

This realization can be sad, but it's part of what happens as you get older. And it leads a whole lot of people to think, "Why does it seem like everyone is moving on except for me?"

This is actually a core fear for a lot of us. You don't want someone to move on and forget about you. You don't want to be left behind in the same old rut you feel stuck in.

Unfortunately, sometimes it's a little bit worse than that.

Maybe it's not that you feel left behind, but you feel abandoned. Cast aside. Intentionally rejected.

You feel forgotten.

> **What are some things that people do (whether they mean to or not) that can make you feel left out?**

It was a hot summer afternoon a few years ago, and I had driven for several hours in a torrential rainstorm, pulling a heavy trailer on the way to a scheduled show.

When I was an hour away, we called the venue but only got the voicemail. We kept trying over and over until we arrived. There, we found the person in charge and asked where we should load in and set up for the show. With a confused look on his face, he replied, "You're not supposed to be here." Apparently, he forgot to call us when he decided to cancel.

I had driven for many hours, spent my own money on gas, and had said no to other offers, all for this one show. But the man forgot to inform me that they no longer wanted me there. I was angry. I was hurt. I was confused.

The pain of being forgotten that day was real. But it was only temporary. Today, we are going to see someone who literally used his final words to express how badly he didn't want to be forgotten. We're going to see who it was that remembered him, and why it is so important for us today, two thousand years later.

ENCOUNTER

> **When has someone done something thoughtful for you?**

> **When you need a pick-me-up—something to help you feel a little more hopeful when you're feeling down—what do you do?**

"Good Friday" has always been a strange name to me. I call it strange because something terrible happened on Good Friday: an innocent man died in the place of a murderer. Here is a four-sentence backstory before we read the passage.

Jesus was arrested on bogus charges, and the law enforcement knew it. So the guy in charge gave the crowd a choice: they could kill Jesus, but it meant setting a murderer free. The crowd cheered. They couldn't wait to kill Jesus instead of Barabbas. So they marched Jesus, an innocent man, up a hill to die.

>> *Have a volunteer read Luke 23:32-38 out loud.*

> **What sticks out to you about Jesus' prayer in verse 34?**

> **Why do you think it's so difficult to have this kind of mentality toward people who hate us?**

When this passage starts, Jesus has had no sleep for an entire day; He was up all night and was arrested early in the morning. He had been betrayed by one of His best friends, arrested for something He didn't do, mocked, sentenced to die, and was now nailed onto a cross He wouldn't leave until He was dead.

So far, there's really not much "good" about this Friday.

Luke tells us that two others were being crucified on that same day. Barabbas, the man Jesus replaced, had killed people during a riot in the city. It's not much of a stretch to think that these two were being killed for the same thing.

They had probably been in prison waiting for their execution date. They probably didn't sleep much the night before, either, but the difference is that they knew what they'd done. They were getting what they deserved.

> **What kinds of regrets do you think people have at the end of their lives?**

As they hung on their own crosses, they knew what had put them there. But imagine their surprise when someone other than Barabbas marched up the hill to die with them. Someone who hadn't done what the people were killing Him for.

I don't know about you, but I would be confused. I want to believe in justice: that people see the consequences of their actions, and innocent people go free. That good people don't get mocked and beaten for no reason.

Let's see how they handled it.

>> **Have a volunteer read verses 39-42 out loud.**

> **What differences do you see in these two men's responses?**

What the second criminal said in verse 42 keeps me up at night. He knew that in a matter of hours, he was going to be dead. Romans were extremely good at killing criminals; there was no way he was getting out alive. Also, he knew what he had done to get there. He admitted as much to his friend.

But here's what gets to me. We have no idea whether he knew who Jesus was or not. Whether he saw Jesus as He walked through the streets. Whether he heard the whispers of the kinds of things Jesus did, the things that people would say about Him with wonder in their breath.

On the other hand, we can be almost certain of what he was most afraid: that he was going to die and be forgotten. That this was the end. After today, he was going to be no more, and nobody in the world would care.

So he did something incredible. He did the same thing the woman from last session did. He took as much faith as he had, and he put it in as much of Jesus as he knew.

What did he know? He knew that Jesus was innocent. He said so. He knew what Jesus was enduring. He could see it with his own eyes. Most importantly, he knew what they were saying to Him: "Save yourself, King of the Jews."

He had nothing left. Nothing to give. Nothing Jesus could use, nothing Jesus needed. So he said the only thing he could think to say: "Jesus, remember me when you come into your kingdom."

» *Have a volunteer read how Jesus responded in verse 43 out loud.*

> **What do you think it means to have faith in Jesus?**

> **How did this criminal demonstrate his faith?**

He was about to be forgotten. Forever. And his last words weren't a desperate plea to be taken off of the cross, to be given a miracle, to wake up and have this all be a bad dream, but to not be forgotten.

And then Jesus spoke. And he wasn't forgotten.

CONNECT

What is so amazing, so good, about that Friday is that it represents the exact moment we became like the thief on the cross. We can be remembered, too. Every one of us. Scooped up and adopted and new.

We don't have to worry about being forgotten and left behind. Because Jesus has already promised to remember anyone who asks Him to.

We've now had two different examples of people in very different situations doing the exact same thing and seeing the exact same result. They put as much faith as they had—even if it was just a raindrop compared to the ocean—in as much of Jesus as they knew—even if it was just a single encounter.

That's what faith in Jesus looks like. It is not a set of magical words or a list of facts you have to memorize. It's what broken, branded, disastrous, invisible, forgotten people do when they see the only one who promises to fix them.

And He is the same today as He was then, waiting for you to say, "Jesus, remember me when you enter your kingdom," so He can say, "you will be with me in paradise."

> **What is the action step you feel the Spirit calling you to take right now?**

>> *Together as a group or on your own, read Psalm 118 and Psalm 136.*

> **Underline or highlight every time you see a promise that God's love endures forever.**

Remember, you are never forgotten. You are loved. His steadfast love endures forever.

Something that I've learned as I've gotten older is that no matter what I'm feeling or thinking, there's usually someone who has felt it or thought it before me. But I wasn't expecting to find this feeling in the place where I found it. I was feeling abandoned by God. Forgotten. Cast aside. Thinking, "God says He cares about me, so why in the world do I feel like He just doesn't anymore?"

Know where I found someone else who felt that way? In the Bible.

Here. Let's do a little exercise. We're going to read a whole chapter right now, and answer some questions about ourselves along the way.

>> **Open your Bible to Psalm 43. Let's begin:**

> *Vindicate me, God, and champion my cause*
> *against an unfaithful nation;*
> *rescue me from the deceitful and unjust person.*
> *For you are the God of my refuge.*
> *Why have you rejected me?*
> *Why must I go about in sorrow*
> *because of the enemy's oppression?*

Which of these lines sticks out to you the most? Why?

Which of these lines have you felt before? Which of them do you feel now?

Send your light and your truth; let them lead me.
Let them bring me to your holy mountain,
to your dwelling place.
Then I will come to the altar of God,
to God, my greatest joy.
I will praise you with the lyre,
God, my God.

> **What are the things that make you feel joy?**

> **Does God make you feel joy? Why or why not?**

Why, my soul, are you so dejected?
Why are you in such turmoil?
Put your hope in God, for I will still praise him,
my Savior and my God.

> **What turmoil are you facing right now?**

> **How do you think that turmoil can be resolved?**

This is a dark psalm. It was written from a bad place. The author was feeling exactly like I was feeling: like God had abandoned him, and he would do anything to feel like he used to feel.

If that, or something like that, describes how you feel, I have extremely good news for you. You are not the first to feel that way, and God has already given us a gift to assure us that we are not forgotten.

In fact, it's the complete opposite. You are not forgotten by God. Not at all. You are loved. And I can't wait to show you how.

In every single place where people live, there are two different categories of folks living there.

One group generally fits in with the rest. They go about their business, walk into the mall and buy things, talk to their friends. They can go most places without much of a second glance. They have on decent clothes, they're doing "regular" stuff like the people around them are doing, and most people would look at them and not really think much of them at all. They're just like the rest of us.

But there's another group of people that doesn't really seem to fit in. People scoot to the other end of the sidewalk when they have to walk by them. They avoid looking them in the eye. You might pass them in the hall and think, *they smell bad*. You might hear the things that they say and think, *well, they're just weird.*

There are people all around us who live on the outskirts of society. They've been rejected. They're not included in our gatherings, and they don't feel welcome in our homes. They don't really fit in. They have been forgotten by "mainstream" society.

We're going to read about one of these people today.

> ***Open your Bible and read Luke 7:36-50.***

If we're going to understand this, we have to read it the way it was meant to be read.

Back then, the only person who was allowed to see a woman's hair was her husband. It was considered an intimate act. A sexual one. And the fact that we see this woman in this passage doing what she did tells us a lot about who she probably was.

She may have been a prostitute. She may have had a dirty reputation. But we know something for certain: she didn't fit in with the crowd. They probably passed her walking into the house and didn't even see her, because she was one of those people who had been forgotten by society.

Look at how Jesus treated her. Not only did He not condemn her, but He actually scolded the Pharisees He was eating with!

She wasn't behaving in a socially acceptable way, but to Jesus that didn't matter. Because the only thing He saw was what she intended: she wanted to show Him how much she loved Him.

Maybe you feel like she did: like an outcast. Maybe you feel like you never do anything the right way. Maybe you've been mistreated and wronged and you just can't understand why—you feel like your heart is in the right place, but no matter what happens, you're cast aside. On the outskirts. In the wrong.

Jesus sees you. More than that, Jesus remembers you. He singles you out even though you feel like people put you off, and He tells you to be at peace. He does all of this for one reason: because He loves you. Exactly as you are.

> **Have you ever felt like an outcast? What are some things about yourself that you wish people knew?**

> **How well do you think "outsiders" like this woman are treated by your friend group? By your city? By your church? What can you do to treat people the way Jesus did?**

In the last study, we saw a woman who didn't really fit in very well with what other people expected of her. I'd even go as far as to say that she had some warped ideas about what love looks like.

But think about how much courage it took for her to approach Jesus exactly as she was. There He sat in a room full of important people, and she had no problem walking in and, without caring what anybody else thought of her, approaching Jesus honestly. She held nothing back. It wasn't perfect, but it was enough.

No matter who you are or what you're like, one of the most important things you can feel is the feeling of belonging somewhere. Like you fit in with the people around you—even if they don't look like you or dress like you or act like you.

> **Where is somewhere you feel like you belong?**

> **Why do you feel that way there?**

> **What do you think makes someone feel like they belong somewhere?**

Making someone feel like they belong is not about forcing them to become exactly like everyone else. It's actually a lot simpler than that. You just have to make them feel welcome and accepted.

That's easy when you're on a sports team or in the same club. Everyone who joins those things already has something in common. You all feel welcome because you have something in common.

But it can get a little bit tricky when we zoom out from that one specific team or club. Suddenly, not everyone has the same interests. They don't have the same backgrounds or experiences. At one point, the church was faced with a tough situation. It suddenly had to make thousands of people, all at once, know they belonged, even though each individual was different.

>> *In your Bible, read Acts 2:41-47.*

Peter had just preached a message, and as a result, three thousand people got saved. How in the world do you make three thousand people feel welcome?

Well, the text tells us. They started sharing everything they had. They had meals together. They helped each other study.

We have a word for this kind of gathering those early believers had: *community.*

Human beings are built for community. God made us that way. One of our most basic needs is to feel like we belong. As members of God's family, we have the chance to show everyone, no matter what they look like or how they dress or how they act, that when they're around us, they are welcome. That they are seen. That they are accepted.

That they are loved.

Do a little audit of your own life:

> **How welcome do you think "outsiders" feel in your friend group? Why?**

> **How welcome do you think they feel in your church? Why?**

> **What things do you think might keep someone from feeling welcomed and accepted by these two groups?**

> **What is something you can do to change that?**

Session 6

SUCCESS

PRESS PLAY

Watch the Session 6 video. Take notes and list any questions in the space below to discuss after with your group.

START

A while back, I had the opportunity to film a TV show at the legendary Dark Horse Recording Studios in Nashville. I spent a whole summer in the recording studio and had time to take a look around. I quickly noticed the plaques on the walls, filled with famous artists who have sold millions of records. There was a picture of Taylor Swift on a wall near the entrance with her multi-platinum record that was recorded there. On the lower level was Dolly Parton with a display celebrating 100 million records sold. That's big, big, big success.

I have a friend who has a room so full of trophies from racing motorcycles that it has become a problem. He doesn't even want them anymore because they just take up space and get dusty. So he's started throwing them away because they have become such a nuisance.

Did you catch that? His trophies became a nuisance. He worked hard, training and racing to accomplish those wins. But a few years later it doesn't even matter to him.

It doesn't matter if you have sold millions of records or won a room full of trophies. None of our success matters in the long run. It can't get us to heaven, it can't deal with our sin, it can't and it won't mean a thing in eternity. Our self-made success is very temporary.

> **What is something you've done that you are most proud of?**

Every now and then, we get one of those moments. They don't come along that often, but you might have had one: your chest fills with pride because you know you have done something truly great.

Maybe you got an A on a test you were sure you were going to fail until you studied relentlessly for a week straight. It might have been getting into an exclusive club. It might have been beating a high score or squeezing out a win at the buzzer.

It is good to have moments like this. It's important to feel proud of yourself for accomplishing something. But there are some problems that could develop from that, too.

Here's one of the problems: you start defining yourself based on these successes. You must keep having them or else your entire perspective of who you are starts to crumble. You become that guy talking about a high school football victory for years to come.

Here's another problem: you start defining yourself the opposite way. You see yourself only as the collection of all of your failures. Your identity, at least in your mind, is linked to only the things you've messed up.

Jesus told a parable that actually addresses both of these things at the same time, but it has been used over the years to say something it doesn't actually mean. What it does mean is honestly pretty mind blowing.

ENCOUNTER

Pharisees. You can hardly go three sentences in the New Testament without hearing about these guys. They're always trying to trap Jesus, He's always using them as sermon illustrations, and they're always causing a stir wherever Jesus goes.

Here's the thing about Pharisees: they were smart. They knew the Law backwards and forwards. Almost literally. Most of the Pharisees probably had most, if not all, of Genesis, Exodus, Leviticus, Numbers, and Deuteronomy completely memorized.

For them, you were only as good as the effort you put in. They got their self-worth from how faithful they had been to keeping God's Law.

By itself, keeping God's Law isn't a problem. But there is a point where it can go too far. One of the Pharisees' main problems with Jesus was that He let sinners be around Him. In their minds, there wasn't anything good that came from hanging out with people who sinned. Jesus was an embarrassment for them.

> **Why do you think it's important to be careful about who we let speak into our lives?**

> **Where do you think the line is between saying, "I try to be careful about who I let influence me" and "I don't associate with people who are sinners"?**

Jesus knew what was on these peoples' hearts. So one day, when He was talking with some tax collectors and other people Pharisees didn't associate with, they came up to Him and started complaining about the company He kept. So He started telling the whole crowd some parables—fictional stories that are told to illustrate a point. The last one, the parable of the prodigal son, is the one that we are going to look at today.

>> *Have a volunteer read Luke 15:11-19 out loud.*

> Think about Jesus' audience: Pharisees, scribes (kind of like religious lawyers), tax collectors, and sinners. How do you think each of these people would have reacted to the younger son's actions in this parable?

This younger son did some bad stuff in the minds of the Pharisees. First, the son asked for his inheritance while his father was still alive—a disrespect to the father. This was basically the son saying he wished his father was dead.

Second, he wasted all of the money he took from his father on foolish living. Third, he became a pig farmer. Pigs were considered unclean by Jews—they weren't supposed to eat them, touch them, or even be near them.

The Pharisees would have been absolutely livid—and they probably couldn't wait to hear the father reject the son's apology.

> What do you think of the apology the son was planning? Does it seem genuine to you? Why or why not?

> What does a genuine apology look like?

Honestly, the apology may or may not have been genuine. We really don't know, and we probably won't have a chance to know. Because Jesus wasn't done with the parable.

>> *Have a volunteer read verses 20-24 out loud.*

> What do you think surprised the Pharisees most about the father's reaction?

> What do you think the other people—the "tax collectors and sinners"—were thinking at this point?

The father reacted in probably the most un-Pharisee way imaginable. There wasn't a single "I told you so." Not one demand for repayment. Not even a hint of anger. When the son who ran away returned, there was nothing but joy. Celebration. A feast. Gift-giving.

But again, Jesus still wasn't done. He hasn't reached the real point of the parable yet.

>> **Have a volunteer read verses 25-32 out loud.**

> In your own words, describe the older son's reaction. How did it make you feel?

> Why do you think Jesus included this section? How did it relate to the people He was telling the parable to?

Here we have it. The older son, who had done everything right, was angry. He couldn't believe what his younger brother did, and he couldn't believe his father's reaction. It was unfair: he had never messed up even once, but their father had never thrown him this kind of feast.

Jesus nailed the Pharisees' attitude down to the letter. They were so caught up with how great they were, how righteously they behaved, how perfect their obedience was, that they forgot what the Law was all about in the first place.

Obedience to the Law was never about checking boxes or making sure you did all the things you were supposed to do. It was about living in community with the Father. About experiencing the joy of His presence every moment of every day. And by making it something it wasn't, they had missed the point entirely.

They were so busy defining themselves by their successes that they forgot the most important thing. They were not their successes. They were loved.

CONNECT

Maybe you're like the Pharisees—the older brother. You define yourself by how good you've been. You think it's unfair when someone who didn't work as hard turns out well. You chase success after success because that's all you even want.

Or maybe you're like the younger brother. You see how much you've failed and you hope that there is some magic combination of words you can say that might make everything right again. Your failure colors the way you see yourself.

This parable shows us that, for both people, the answer is the same. It is found in the Father's steadfast love. Nobody is too far gone to come back, and His grace covers everyone, regardless of whether you're a "success" or a "failure."

No matter where you stand, God will run to meet you on the road, because He is like the father in the parable. He's watching you return, broken.

He is there. For you. Because you are so deeply, incredibly loved.

> **Which of the two brothers do you feel describes you the most? Why?**

> **How does the fact that God loves you exactly where you are affect the way that you see yourself?**

The parable of the prodigal son is one of my favorite parables Jesus told. In this week's group session, you talked about something that might have felt a little personal:

> **Which son are you most like? Are you the younger son or the older son?**

This is an important question, because most of us fit one of the descriptions pretty well. Some of us have felt far away from God because of choices we've made. Feeling like a failure. Like we will never be able to do enough to get back to Him.

But some of us see ourselves in the older son. We are defined by our successes. Like we've done enough to earn our spot with God. Like we deserve good things and we deserve God's favor because of how great we are.

Let's drill down a little further into this idea to help us understand a little more about what it means to be defined by God—not by what we have done.

Rate how well each of these statements describes you on a scale from 1 to 10.

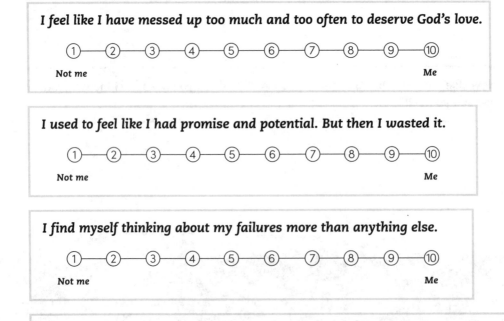

I feel like I have messed up too much and too often to deserve God's love.

①—②—③—④—⑤—⑥—⑦—⑧—⑨—⑩

Not me   Me

I used to feel like I had promise and potential. But then I wasted it.

①—②—③—④—⑤—⑥—⑦—⑧—⑨—⑩

Not me   Me

I find myself thinking about my failures more than anything else.

①—②—③—④—⑤—⑥—⑦—⑧—⑨—⑩

Not me   Me

When I think about myself, the first word that comes to mind is "imperfect."

①—②—③—④—⑤—⑥—⑦—⑧—⑨—⑩

Not me   Me

Now consider how well each of these statements describes you on a scale from 1 to 10.

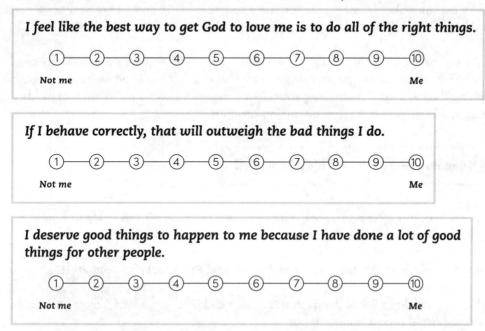

I feel like the best way to get God to love me is to do all of the right things.

① — ② — ③ — ④ — ⑤ — ⑥ — ⑦ — ⑧ — ⑨ — ⑩

Not me   *Me*

If I behave correctly, that will outweigh the bad things I do.

① — ② — ③ — ④ — ⑤ — ⑥ — ⑦ — ⑧ — ⑨ — ⑩

Not me   *Me*

I deserve good things to happen to me because I have done a lot of good things for other people.

① — ② — ③ — ④ — ⑤ — ⑥ — ⑦ — ⑧ — ⑨ — ⑩

Not me   *Me*

No matter where you fall, God has the same thing to say to you: "You are not loved more or less because of the things you have done. You are loved simply because I love you."

As you bring your personal study time to a close, revisit the parable of the prodigal son in Luke 15:11-32. Then, in the space below, jot down your reaction to how the father in the parable responded to each son.

Which reaction makes you feel most uplifted? Why?

Which reaction would you most like to hear?

What do they each tell you about what God is like?

For just about as long as human beings have been thinking, they've been trying to figure out what makes a good life. For some, a good life is one where you have everything you need. For others, life is good when you have only the best.

One person might think that a good life is one where you enjoy as many things as you possibly can. Another person might think that a good life is one where you build something that will last. There are probably as many answers for "What makes life meaningful?" as there are people walking around.

> **What do you think makes life meaningful?**

Today, we're going to see someone who reflected back on his life to try to figure out what the answer to that question was.

>> *In your Bible, find Ecclesiastes (after Psalms and Proverbs) and read 2:4-11.*

Look at the incredible list of things that this man did. His name was Solomon, and he was one of Israel's most famous kings.

And from what we just read, he had just about everything. Wealth and wisdom. Pleasure and plenty. He had people working for him. He had a legacy. He even said, "If I ever saw anything that I wanted, I got it."

Can you imagine what that's like? There was nothing he lacked. Nothing he failed to understand. He had, quite literally, everything.

So isn't the end of that passage a little strange? How in the world could someone with a list of accomplishments like Solomon tell us, after what may seem a little bit like a humblebrag, that everything was meaningless?

These are the things that people want. They're what people work their whole lives for. Money and pleasure and peace and comfort are things that every single person wants! How could he say it's meaningless?

It seems a little depressing. In fact, many people keep reading the rest of that book and feel overwhelmed by what he says. "If everything is meaningless, what actually matters?"

Solomon eventually got there. In the second-to-last verse of the whole book. This is the conclusion that he reached: "When all has been heard, the conclusion of the matter is this: fear God and keep his commands, because this is for all humanity" (Ecc. 12:13).

Solomon, one of the richest people in history, said that riches didn't mean a single thing. The only thing that mattered was fearing—or loving—God.

When we start defining ourselves by our successes—or even our failures—we're defining ourselves by something that eventually goes away. You got a lot of money? Great. Money goes away. You keep messing up? That's alright. It'll be forgotten in no time.

The only thing that won't fade away, though, is the one who made us. Solomon's teaching is clear: love Him and obey Him. The rest of that stuff will come and go, but God will not.

Do you want to live a life of meaning? A life that is good? Then follow the advice of the person who had it all. Invest in your relationship with your Creator. Everything else will come and go, but He never will.

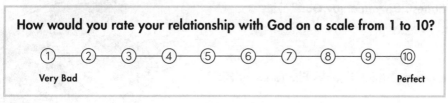

How would you rate your relationship with God on a scale from 1 to 10?

①——②——③——④——⑤——⑥——⑦——⑧——⑨——⑩
Very Bad   **Perfect**

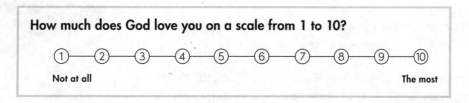

How much does God love you on a scale from 1 to 10?

①——②——③——④——⑤——⑥——⑦——⑧——⑨——⑩
Not at all   **The most**

On a scale from 1-10, God loves you an 11. It's always more than you can imagine. And it is never based on your life. It's based on His life, crucified for you. You are loved.

Think back to the story that Jesus told of the prodigal son—specifically about what the father said at the very end:

> *"You are always with me, and everything I have is yours. But we had to celebrate and rejoice, because this brother of yours was dead and is alive again; he was lost and is found"* (Luke 15:31-32).

We don't know how the older son reacted to his father saying that. But we do know something for sure: both of the sons, whether it was the one who ran away and defined himself by his failures or the older one who stayed and defined himself by his successes, were now in the exact same place. They now had the chance to live in their father's house, be near him, and enjoy his love for the rest of their lives.

Jesus told that parable to lost and broken people, but He included someone in it who wasn't lost and broken. The father represents God. And what the father said to the older son is the exact same thing that He says to you, no matter which of the sons you identify with the most.

You have the same opportunity those sons had. You get the chance to be with the Father. To love Him. To enjoy Him.

> **Be honest. Do you enjoy God?**

> **What do you think it looks like to enjoy Him?**

> **What do you think it would take for you to enjoy Him?**

One of the greatest gifts God gave us was His Word. We've read it in every single one of these sessions. In it, He tells us what He is like and how to know Him best.

Look at one of the ways He wants us to do that.

Psalm 46:10 says, "Be still, and know that I am God" (NIV).

Be still.

Here's what "be still" means. Just for a second, stop thinking about what you have to do to earn His love. Stop thinking about all of the steps you need to take to get back to Him. Take a minute to settle, to sit, to reflect and know what has been there the whole time: the God who loves you. The God who sees you. The God who has sealed you.

Let me walk you through a really easy process you can do at any time to help you be still. Try it right now.

1. **Sit somewhere like a window or on a bench outside.** Look at everything around you. God made this. It reflects little pieces of Him.

> **Ask yourself: What is something I can see right now that is beautiful? Very briefly, thank God for it.**

2. **As you are sitting, take stock of your thoughts.** What are you feeling? What is troubling you? What are you ashamed of?

> **Ask yourself: What is something I can let Jesus take off my plate? Very briefly, ask God to ease you where you are troubled.**

3. **Finally, think about some of the things that you have.** They could be tangible things, like a house, or something else, like healthy relationships.

> **Ask yourself: What is something I am thankful for? Very briefly, thank God for it.**

It may be difficult at first, but you'll get the hang of it. You'll get used to being still, and as you do, you'll get used to listening for what God is saying to you. Because it doesn't matter which of the sons in the parable you are, you have the same Father: the Father who tells you that it doesn't matter to Him whether you are a success or a failure, He loves you exactly the same. You are loved.

Session 7

LOVED

PRESS PLAY

Watch the Session 7 video. Take notes and list any questions in the space below to discuss after with your group.

START

I love ice cream. I love my wife. I love riding motorcycles. I love my family.

Do you see the odd contrast there? They are so different, yet I use the word *love* to describe each one. Love seems so inadequate to describe what I feel for my family when I compare it to, say, ice cream.

So what is love? Are there different kinds of love?

The problem is we use one word to describe things that have different meanings. But there is only one type of love we are talking about here: it's a high-level, high-commitment kind of love. It's not the kind of love you use for your favorite color or favorite food. No, the kind of love I'm talking about is called *agape* love.

This is the limitless, unconditional, and perfect love. This is the love that's missing in our lives. This is the love that our hearts yearn for. This is the kind of love that is only truly satisfied in a relationship with Christ.

Jesus exemplified this love by dying on a cross for us. Even though we were sinners, He acted first and willingly died in our place so that we can have eternal life in fellowship with Him. He loves us unconditionally, without fault, and completely. When we mess up, He still loves us. When we feel broken, invisible, like a disaster or a failure, He still loves us more than we can comprehend. We can always know that His steadfast agape love will endure forever.

When Jesus was being arrested, a group of men came for Him. During the altercation, Peter, a close friend and disciple of Jesus, pulled out a sword and swung it at the servant of the high priest (John 18:10). The guy ducked and turned, but the sword caught his ear, cutting it clean off. What happened next is the most incredible display of Christ's love.

Jesus bent over, picked up the man's ear, and put it back on his head (Luke 22:51). The man who had the authority to arrest Jesus on false charges stood still long enough for Jesus to heal his ear. Jesus showed love to the one arresting Him.

As Jesus was taking His final few breaths on the cross, He looked down at the men who had nailed His hands and feet onto the wooden cross. He watched them gamble for His clothes and said, "Father, forgive them" (Luke 23:34). Even in the middle of such pain, He loved the very ones still holding hammers and nails in their hands.

> **When was a time you genuinely felt loved?**

The feeling you get when you get done telling someone about a problem you have and they look you in the eye and tell you, "OK. Let's tackle it together."

Or when your friend approaches you and says, "Hey. You look more stressed out than normal. Do you want to talk about it?"

Or when you open a gift and it isn't an expensive gadget or a generic card, but a thought-out, handmade reference to an inside joke only you two know.

It overwhelms you. Fills you up from the inside. Makes your chest warm and your burdens light. You feel it up and down your spine: "I am loved."

> **What makes you feel the most loved and cherished?**

If you walk away from this book and immediately forget everything, or decide it's not for you, I hope that, at the very least, you have one simple sentence that echoes in your brain.

If you take absolutely nothing away from any of this except for one statement, let it be this: I am loved.

Let me prove it to you.

ENCOUNTER

> **Over the last few weeks, we've seen a lot of people who found out in different ways that they were loved by Jesus. Who stuck out to you most? Why?**

It's helpful for us to read about people who got to see how much Jesus loved them in person. They got to touch His hands. Hear His voice. But sometimes, that doesn't cut it for us. We need something else.

>> **Have a volunteer read Ephesians 2:1-3 out loud.**

> **What do you think "sin" means?**

> **What do you think the text means when it says "the inclinations of our flesh and thoughts"?**

Before we can see exactly what it means to know how loved we are, we first have to sort of understand why it's a big deal in the first place.

It is easy to say "sin" and then think of a laundry list of "bad stuff." Sin is lying, cheating, and stealing. Of course, we could call those things sins, because they are. But sin is so much bigger than that.

Think about it like this. God created each and every one of us for two things and two things only. To glorify Him and enjoy Him forever. It's why He walked with Adam in the garden of Eden. It's why He told them to multiply and fill the earth with more people who could do the same. We were created to be in community with God—to have Him on the throne of our hearts.

But somewhere along the line, our thrones got a little bit confused. It's in our nature to get our thrones confused. We put other things up there: success, image, experiences, enjoyment, our relationships—ourselves.

Sin is simple: it is us telling God that He is not the one on the throne. We've replaced Him.

Sometimes that looks like lying. Sometimes it looks like stealing. But it's always more than just an action—it is an attitude. You'd think that this would make God angry. And, well, it does. He's the King, and we are so good at making Him *not* the King.

Stop. Remember our mantra. Remember the one sentence that I want you to remember. *You are loved.* Look at how much.

» *Have a volunteer continue reading verses 4-10 out loud.*

> **How difficult do you think it is to love someone who is constantly telling you that you're not important? Why?**

> **How does this passage tell us God showed His love for us?**

This same author, Paul, told a different church something similar: "Christ died for the ungodly. ... While we were still sinners, Christ died for us" (Rom. 5:6,8).

Think back to what the thief on the cross with Jesus heard Him say: "Father, forgive them, because they do not know what they are doing" (Luke 23:34).

How could He even say that? Look at what they'd done to Him! He was dying a criminal's death even though He wasn't a criminal. He physically took the place of someone else who was supposed to be on that cross.

But this passage is telling us that He did it for us. He did it to pay the tab that we had racked up. He did it to cover every expense we owed. God is our King, and we constantly betray Him—but instead of letting us die for it (even though we deserve it), Jesus said, "I'll die instead. They don't owe anything anymore."

Let me put it another way. Even though our sin breaks God's heart, He loved us so much that He gave us a way to get back to Him. He didn't cut us off. He didn't forsake us or leave us behind.

We are not invisible to Him. We're not forgotten by Him. We're not broken failures—we are loved and cherished and purchased.

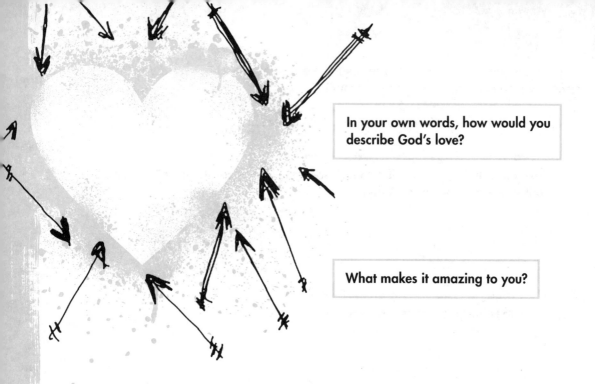

In your own words, how would you describe God's love?

What makes it amazing to you?

God's love is like nothing we can even understand, because He is like nothing we can understand. But something about His love that we can understand is that it lasts forever.

In John 10:27-28, Jesus said, "My sheep hear my voice, I know them, and they follow me. I give them eternal life, and they will never perish. No one will snatch them out of my hand."

Let that sink in. *No one will snatch them out of my hand.*

That includes you. If you have done as so many others have done and thrown yourself at Jesus' feet, saying, "I'm imperfect and I don't deserve it, but I'm yours," you are His forever.

And if you haven't done that, God loves you so much that He has given you the chance to. Right now. Right this second.

Because you, no matter who you are, are loved.

>> **Read Psalm 136 out loud as a group.**

Take a few minutes to think of some other things to add to that list. What is something that God has done to show you that He loves you?

God's love is a thread that weaves throughout history, back to the very beginning. Back to when the Creator of the universe looked at what He made. He didn't say:

"It is broken" or
"It is only as good as it can make itself" or
"It is a disaster" or
"It isn't worth being seen" or
"It is forgettable" or
"It is the sum of its successes and failures."

He said, "It is very good."

Because it—you—are. And you are so loved.

CONNECT

Before your last session ends, I want you to do one last thing. Get to a spot where you can be alone and quiet, and set a timer for five minutes. By yourself, read Psalm 139:1-16 slowly and quietly.

Then, with the time that is left, sit. Just sit. You don't have to do anything or go anywhere, or talk to anyone, just sit and reflect on the most important thing you will ever hear in your life.

You. Are. Loved.

I don't have to convince you that we know exactly what it's like to have to earn things.

If you are an athlete and you want to win a championship, you know that you're going to have to earn it. Not in the big game—before. In the months and years of practice leading up to it.

If you want a good grade on a test, you're going to have to earn it. Not during the test itself, but in the weeks spent studying and listening and learning.

"Earn it" is so ingrained in us that it carves rivers in our hearts. It bleeds over into everything from relationships to friendships to the whole plan for our lives. We live with the expectation that if we want something to be good, we have to earn it.

This is generally true. But where we get it completely wrong is with God. Somehow, we get the impression that if God is going to love us, we have to earn it.

First John 4:19 tells us that "we love because [God] first loved us." He did it first. He loves us without us having to do a single thing to earn it. He loves us despite the terrible things we've done. He loves us even though we will fail Him. Over and over and over.

If we try to approach God with the mentality of having to earn His love, we start missing things. We miss the beauty of sitting in His presence. We miss the joy of knowing that He's there—and that it isn't changing because of something we do. We miss the safety of the refuge that can be found in His arms. We miss the fullness of the life He promises all the people who put their trust in Him.

Too often, we find ourselves working for God's love. I think we need to reverse that.

Instead of working for God's love, what if we started working from it?

What if, in a world that is changing all the time, we approached each day from the same foundational knowledge: "God loves me"?

What if, when it seems like everything is falling apart, we could resort to the only thing we know is true: "God loves me"?

What if, whenever we're feeling inadequate, disastrous, invisible, the only thing we remember is, "God loves me"?

It would probably change some things, don't you think?

> *How does "God loves me" affect the way that you see yourself?*

> *How does "God loves me" affect the way that you see others?*

> *How does "God loves me" affect the way that you see Him?*

I don't know if there's anything in this world more misunderstood than love.

We're told a million different things from a million different places. Some of you might have been told, "I love you," only to be hurt by that person over and over. Some of you might have heard, "If you loved me, you would _____."

Some equate love with sex. With selflessness. With favors. With a checklist of things that go along with such a big, heavy word like love.

Then, at the same time, we talk about other things that we love. Books. Movies. Outfits. Activities. Theme parks. Talking about love sometimes feels like talking about the ocean: we can describe it, we can talk about the things it contains, but whenever we try to hold it, it slips through our fingers.

> **In your own words, what do you think love is?**

> **Who are some people in your life that you love?**

Paul tried to put together a little bit of a description of what love is. What love looks like. What love does.

>> *In your Bible, read what he wrote in 1 Corinthians 13:1-8. Stop at "Love never ends."*

In the first part of that passage, Paul described some amazing things. Talking in the tongues of angels. Giving everything he has to the poor. Having incredible understanding. But he says, "If I have those things and don't have love, I have nothing at all."

Because love goes deeper than *what* we do. Love is about *why* we do it. Do you want to know if it's love? The second half of that verse shows us the things that love looks like.

> **Read the list in verses 4-7 again. Which of these things sticks out to you the most? Why?**

> **Have you ever known someone who looks the way this verse describes? Who was it? What were they like?**

> **Do you think someone could describe you this way?**

Maybe you're like me, and you read this list and think, "I wish someone would love me that way."

Fortunately, someone has. We read this passage in the main session, but look at it one more time:

> *"God proves his own love for us in that while we were still sinners, Christ died for us"* (Rom. 5:8).

» Christ looked at the people who spat in His face and said, "I love you."

» He looked at the people who drove nails into His wrists and said, "I love you."

» He looked at the people society had cast away and said, "I love you."

» He looked at the people who were self-righteous and pompous and said, "I love you."

And Christ looks at you, exactly where you are, with every one of your imperfections and flaws and insecurities and doubts and sins and says the exact same thing.

I love you.

> **What is something you need to do in response to Christ's love for you?**

> **Who is one person in your life that you can focus on loving better?**

You have come to the end of the study. This is it. It's the last day. And we have covered some serious ground.

> **What are a couple of things from the video sessions that stuck out to you?**

> **What are a couple of things from your group time that stuck out to you?**

I don't know exactly what you are going through right now. What you're struggling with. But I do know one thing: God is bigger than any of it. It is nothing that He hasn't seen before, and it is nothing that He won't love you through.

More than anything, I want you to know how to keep knowing Him better and better, even when you don't have someone walking you through it. Last week, we learned how to take a moment out of your day, to be still, and to just sit. Today, we're going to see how to read His Word on our own.

You can really start anywhere, but I'm going to recommend starting with the Gospel of John as you get the hang of what I'm about to show you. Once a day, read just one single chapter. Then, when you're done reading that chapter, get out a notebook and follow these four steps:

> **Highlight a verse that really stood out to you when you read it. Write that verse down on the page. If you want, you can even copy it out.**

> **Explain the context of that verse.**

This sounds scary, but it isn't. All you're doing is writing down a sentence or two about how that verse fits in with the rest of the verses in the chapter. Maybe what led up to it or what follows it.

You don't have to make an earth-shaking revelation or anything like that, but in just a couple of sentences, write down how you think it applies to you.

Respond to God.

This might look like writing down a way to practice what the verse told you to do. It might look like writing out a short prayer to God. It might look like writing an action step to remember as you go throughout your day.

That's it. If you can do those four things, you can continue what we have already started in this study. And as you do it more and more, you're going to start realizing something that will absolutely change your life.

The Creator of the universe knows you, sees you, longs for you, and loves you. There is nothing you can do, nothing you could have been, no way you can feel about yourself, that will change this.

You are not broken. You are not a brand. You are not a disaster. You are not invisible. You are not forgotten. You are not your successes and failures.

You are, simply, loved.

LEADER GUIDE

Thank you for your commitment to lead students. It is our hope and prayer that God will use this study to help students understand that they don't have to be perfect in order to receive God's love. The Leader Guide is designed to help you prepare for each session and equip you with additional tools, questions, and activities as you lead students to understand the impact of an encounter with Jesus.

HOW DOES THE LEADER GUIDE WORK?

The Leader Guide is broken up into four short sections:

1. Start   2. Press Play   3. Encounter   4. Connect

START

We've included the main topic of each session at the beginning of each Leader Guide to help you stay focused and on task. We recommend reading the Scripture and reviewing the Group Discussion pages before meeting with students. This section will also give you some tips for opening the session through ice breakers, illustrations, or simple activities that introduce the main point of each session.

PRESS PLAY

After beginning your time together, you will simply press play and watch each session's video with your students. Make sure your video system is set up and working prior to each session.

ENCOUNTER

This section covers the main portion of the group discussion. As you work through these pages together, students will be reading passages and answering questions based on the passage in order to better understand the stories of how lives were changed after an encounter with Jesus.

CONNECT

This section provides a challenge for students to either work on together as a group or alone over the next week. There are a couple different ways you can approach this section. You may want to encourage students to take their books home and complete this section on their own. Groups with more time, however, may decide to have students complete this section at the end of each group meeting.

SESSION 1
BROKEN

This week's lesson is about Jesus' encounter with the Samaritan woman at the well. Read the story in advance so you're prepared to lead the conversation, and make notes beforehand about the things you want to discuss.

START

Welcome students and start with a quick activity to break the ice. Bring a ball and explain that when someone tosses it to you, you have to share something that makes you unique. Share an interesting fact about yourself, then toss it to someone else and continue playing until everyone has a chance to share.

PRESS PLAY

Ask someone to pray, then watch the video for Session 1. Take notes as you watch and be prepared to follow up with specific questions students may have or invite a volunteer to share something that stuck out to them.

ENCOUNTER

Walk through the group discussion starting on page 8, using the discussion questions to generate conversation as you go. Encourage students to read the passages aloud as you discuss the story of Jesus and the woman at the well.

CONNECT

Before you go, use the Connect questions on page 13 to launch students into the week. If they don't feel comfortable answering out loud,

don't pressure them—just tell them to think about it.

Close in prayer and remind students to complete the three personal studies before the next group meeting.

Throughout the week, text each person in the group and remind them that you're praying for them and look forward to seeing them next week.

SESSION 2
BRAND

This week's lesson is about Nicodemus. Read the story in advance so you're prepared to lead the conversation, and make notes beforehand about the things you want to discuss.

START

Start with a quick activity. Bring a few brand-name items with you: some Nike shoes, an iPhone, some M&Ms, a pack of Kleenex, and so on. Lay them out and ask the group what they associate with each brand. Coolness? Reliability? Fun? Press them to explain why and start a conversation about what we look for in the brands we use.

PRESS PLAY

Bring everyone back together and ask if anyone has any questions or wants to share anything they learned in their personal study during the week. Ask someone to pray, then watch the video for Session 2.

ENCOUNTER

Walk through the group discussion starting on page 22, using the discussion questions to generate conversation as you go. Encourage students to read the passages aloud as you discuss Nicodemus's encounter with Jesus.

CONNECT

Before you go, use the Connect questions on page 27 to launch students into the week. If they don't feel comfortable answering out loud, don't pressure them—just tell them to think about it. Bring some index cards and pens and have students write down a few words that they would use to describe the personal "brand" they've been cultivating. Then have them write some words describing a life focused on Christ. What is the difference?

Close in prayer and remind students to complete the three personal studies before the next group meeting.

SESSION 3
DISASTER

This week's lesson is about Zacchaeus. Read the story in advance so you're prepared to lead the conversation, and make notes beforehand about the things you want to discuss.

START

Kick things off with a Rock Paper Scissors tournament: each person in the group chooses a partner to square off against. Then line everyone up across from each other to compete in a best two-out-of-three—winners advance and the losers get to pick someone to cheer on, culminating in a rowdy final showdown. The winner can either get bragging rights or a small prize. (You can't go wrong with candy.)

PRESS PLAY

Bring everyone back together and ask if anyone has any questions or wants to share anything they learned in their personal study during the week. Ask someone to pray, then watch the video for Session 3.

ENCOUNTER

Walk through the group discussion starting on page 36, using the discussion questions to generate conversation as you go. Encourage students to read the passages aloud as you discuss the story of Zacchaeus.

CONNECT

Before you go, use the Connect questions on page 41 to launch students into the week. If they don't feel comfortable answering out loud, don't pressure them—just tell them to think about it. Then, at the bottom of the page, have students write down the name of someone in their lives they will commit to praying for this week.

Close in prayer and remind students to complete the three personal studies before the next group meeting.

SESSION 4
INVISIBLE

This week's lesson is about Jesus' healing of the sick woman. Read the story in advance so you're prepared to lead the conversation, and make notes beforehand about the things you want to discuss.

START

Start with a game of "One Word at a Time." Build a sentence by having each person in the circle say one word at a time. Have someone call out a general topic (sports or food, for instance), then choose a student to kick things off with a single word. Go around the group until you've finished a complete (and unexpected) sentence. Play for a few rounds and see how surprising it can get.

PRESS PLAY

Bring everyone back together and ask if anyone has any questions or wants to share anything they learned in their personal study during the week. Ask someone to pray, then watch the video for Session 4.

ENCOUNTER

Walk through the group discussion starting on page 50, using the discussion questions to generate conversation as you go. Encourage students to read the passages aloud as you discuss the story of Jesus' encounter with the sick woman.

CONNECT

Before you go, use the Connect questions on page 55 to launch students into the week. If they don't feel comfortable answering out loud, don't pressure them—just tell them to think about it. Challenge each student to post a Bible verse or something else they learned on social media this week (and make sure you follow them so you can hold them accountable).

Close in prayer and remind students to complete the three personal studies before the next group meeting.

SESSION 5
FORGOTTEN

This week's lesson is about Jesus' encounter with the criminal on the cross. Read the story in advance so you're prepared to lead the conversation, and make notes beforehand about the things you want to discuss.

START

Start with a game of Would You Rather: Designate one half of the room as Choice A and the other as Choice B. Think of 8-10 questions and have students walk to the side of the room that corresponds to their answer. Mountain Dew or Dr Pepper? Chinese or Mexican food? Get creative, then ask the group to come up with some of their own.

PRESS PLAY

Bring everyone back together and ask if anyone has any questions or wants to share anything they learned in their personal study during the week. Ask someone to pray, then watch the video for Session 5.

ENCOUNTER

Walk through the group discussion starting on page 64, using the discussion questions to generate conversation as you go. Encourage students to read the passages aloud as you discuss the story of Jesus' encounter with the criminal on the cross.

CONNECT

Before you go, use the Connect questions on page 69 to launch students into the week. If they don't feel comfortable answering out loud, don't pressure them—just tell them to think about it. At the bottom, have students write down the names of three people they will pray for this week: One should be a leader in their church, one should be a family member, and one should be a friend or classmate.

Close in prayer and remind students to complete the three personal studies before the next group meeting.

SESSION 6
SUCCESS

This week's lesson is about the parable of the prodigal son. Read the story in advance so you're prepared to lead the conversation, and make notes beforehand about the things you want to discuss.

START

Pass out paper and pens to everyone. Give students five minutes to draw a picture that describes who they are without using any words or numbers. Then, collect the pictures and show them to the group. Have everyone guess who each one represents. Don't forget to do one for yourself!

PRESS PLAY

Bring everyone back together and ask if anyone has any questions or wants to share anything they learned in their personal study during the week. Ask someone to pray, then watch the video for Session 6.

ENCOUNTER

Walk through the group discussion starting on page 78, using the discussion questions to generate conversation as you go. Encourage students to read the passages aloud as you discuss the parable of the lost son.

CONNECT

Before you go, use the Connect questions on page 83 to launch students into the week. If they don't feel comfortable answering out loud, don't pressure them—just tell them to think about it. Tell students to think about the three sections from this discussion: Start, Encounter, and Connect. What do they need to start doing in their walk with Christ? Where can they look to encounter Him this week? How can they connect with him more deeply?

Close in prayer and remind students to complete the three personal studies before the next group meeting.

SESSION 7
LOVED

This week's lesson is about Ephesians 1. Read the passage in advance so you're prepared to lead the conversation, and make notes beforehand about the things you want to discuss.

START

Divide into groups of three. Have students look back at each of the six sessions: Broken, Brand, Disaster, Invisible, Forgotten, and Success. Each one describes a way we see ourselves that God says is not true. Can they come up with any more? Give them the prompt: I am not _____. Offer up one or two (my grades or my job, for instance), then give them a few minutes to talk it over. Ask if anyone wants to share when they're done.

PRESS PLAY

Bring everyone back together and ask if anyone has any questions or wants to share anything they learned in their personal study during the week. Ask someone to pray, then watch the video for Session 7.

ENCOUNTER

Walk through the group discussion starting on page 92, using the discussion questions to generate conversation as you go. Encourage students to read the passages aloud as you discuss God's love for us.

CONNECT

Before you go, do the last group activity in the Connect section on page 97. When students are done reflecting, bring everyone back together and thank them for their commitment to the group. Close in prayer, thanking God for your group and how He's working in their lives. Consider meeting together one more time to celebrate completing the study (potentially with pizza) and to discuss the final pages of personal study.

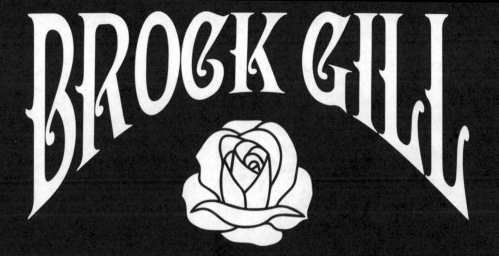

Get the most from your study.

Customize your Bible study time with a guided experience and additional resources.

Join illusionist Brock Gill on a seven-week journey as he uncovers the illusions we believe about ourselves and challenges students to see themselves instead as God sees them: not broken or invisible, but loved. Through the artistry of illusion and his unique gift of evangelism, Brock Gill examines the stories of broken, forgotten, branded, and lost people in the Bible whose lives were forever changed through an encounter with Jesus.

Through daily practice and perseverance, students will be able to discern the truth of God's Word from the confusing messages of today's culture. Creative video segments that incorporate Gill's unique artistry will help students connect the theme for each session to Scripture. And at the end of the seven weeks, students will have experienced personal spiritual growth through individual time spent in Bible study with the content.

Featuring Gill's mind-bending illusions, this video-enhanced Bible study will equip students to encounter Jesus in a way that reveals their eternal worth.

Lifeway designs trustworthy experiences that fuel ministry. Today, the ministries of Lifeway reach more than 160 countries around the globe. For specific information on Lifeway Students, visit lifeway.com/students.

ADDITIONAL RESOURCES

DON'T BELIEVE YOUR EYES: TEEN BIBLE STUDY LEADER KIT
Weekly videos, Bible study book, and additional elements to accompany group sessions and assist leaders (9781087734057)

DON'T BELIEVE YOUR EYES: eBOOK
A digital version of the seven-week study for students and leaders (9781087734033)